Also by Jean Dutourd

A DOG'S HEAD
THE BEST BUTTER
FIVE A.M.
THE TAXIS OF THE MARNE

The Man

Translated from the French
by Robin Chancellor

Simon and Schuster

of *ensibility*

by Jean Dutourd

New York 1961

For Camille, another sensitive soul

❦❦❦❦ *Soul*

The soul is what refuses the body. What, for instance, refuses to flee when the body trembles, what refuses to strike when the body is provoked, what refuses to drink when the body thirsts, what refuses to take when the body desires, what refuses to give up when the body recoils in horror. These refusals are the prerogative of man. Total refusal is sainthood; looking before leaping is wisdom; and this power of refusal is the soul. The madman has no power of refusal; he no longer has a soul. They also say he has no awareness, and that is true. Whoever yields completely to his body, be it to strike, be it to flee, be it merely to speak, no longer knows what he does nor what he is saying. One acquires awareness only through opposing self to self. For example, Alexander while crossing a desert receives a helmet filled with water; he gives thanks and then pours it onto the ground before the whole army. Magnanimity, soul—that is, great soul. There is no such thing as a base soul; only a lack of soul. This beautiful word in no way defines a being, but always an act.

—ALAIN, *Définitions*

✵✵✵✵✵ *Explanation*

So far as I know, there exist three versions of Mérimée's essay on Henri Beyle ("H.B."), better known as Stendhal. One appears at the beginning of the Correspondance inédite; *a second forms part of a collection entitled* Portraits historiques et littéraires, *where it keeps company with studies of Cervantes, Henri de Guise, Victor Jacquemont, Nodier, Brantôme, Pushkin and others, all admirable for the simplicity with which their author expresses extremely subtle thoughts; the third is a small volume on its own called* H.B. par un des Quarante.* *This last is the most successful; in it one finds amusing variations, suppressions and additions. The first printing (twenty-five copies) dates from 1850. It was tempting to take this one for my text;† but I have preferred the second one, in which there are repetitions and careless slips, in which the thought is almost entirely unpolished and in which one finds a number of spontaneous phrases and some touching details. H.B. does great honor to two men I love. It also shows an essential aspect of Stendhal's character, the spirit of contradiction, and, through the example of that*

---

* *I.e. "Henri Beyle by one of the Forty [members of the Académie Française]."*—Tr.

† *The italicized passages at the head of each chapter follow the text of H.B. paragraph by paragraph.*

writer, provides several maxims which are applicable today.

Following a formula dear to Mérimée, his essay begins with a reference to Homer. One finds many such beginnings in his works; they are stylistic niceties. Mérimée was fond of playing the pedant; as such he was the best of company. And what an exquisite discord, to embark on Carmen, for instance, the most savage story in French literature, with a few comments on archaeology, as if this were the author's real interest! It makes the tale that follows seem like a trivial anecdote told to amuse the ladies.

There is a passage in The Odyssey *which comes back to me. The ghost of Elpenor appears to Ulysses and asks to be given funeral honors:*

μη μ᾿κλαυτον, ἀθαπτον ἰων ὄπιθεν καταλέιπειν

Do not leave me unmourned, unburied.

Today, thanks to police regulations, everyone gets buried; but we pagans also have duties to fulfill toward our dead, which do not consist solely of complying with a regulation of the municipal government. I have attended three pagan funerals: that of Sautelet, who blew his brains out (his master, that great philosopher Cousin, and his friends were afraid of respectable opinion and dared not speak); that of M. Jacquemont, who had forbidden any speeches; lastly, that of Beyle. There were three of us present, and so unprepared were we that we did not know what his last wishes might have been. On each occasion I felt that we had neglected something, if not toward the deceased, at least toward ourselves. If one of our friends dies on a journey, we have a sharp pang of regret at not having said goodbye to him before he set out. A departure, a death, should be celebrated with a certain ceremony, for there is something solemn about them. Even were it only a meal, or a regular association of thoughts, something must be done. This something is what Elpenor asks for; he is demanding not only a few feet of earth but also a memory.

I am writing the following pages to make up for what we failed to do at Beyle's funeral. I would like to share my impressions and my memories with some of his friends.

EVEN THOUGH Mérimée leaves little to chance, one must not look for too many intentions in a piece of writing. Elpenor, Ulysses' companion, was not a very shining character. "The least brave in battle, the least wise in counsel," and rather given to drink—so Homer describes him. This imbecile was sleeping it off on the roof of the Temple of Circe. Waking up with a start, he forgot where he was, stumbled forward and fell from the roof, breaking his neck. There could hardly be a stupider way to die.

A living clown may make a terrifying ghost. The dead Elpenor is more substanial than the living Elpenor. His phantom, walking the sea, has a certain pungency. While he remains familiar and well disposed, readily confessing that he owes his demise to one too many, his soul has already undergone various tribulations and become ennobled by misfortunes incomprehensible to mortals. It has wandered to the gates of Hades, it can see into the future; it demands that the body which contained it be burned.

"Raise on my tomb the oar with which I rowed when I dwelt among you!" Elpenor says to Ulysses, thereby meaning that even if his position in life was humble he occupied it nonetheless with dignity and is entitled to have a small monument raised to him on his own small scale. Ulysses, who no doubt felt neither particular esteem nor affection for Elpenor, addresses his spirit with respect and emotion. Things are now quite different: the simple sailor has become in a way a *thought,* or a feeling of remorse; Ulysses has to appease Elpenor's ancestral shades or the thing will lie heavy on his own soul. This is a religious sentiment. Mérimée felt it in the same way, despite his atheism. The world does not begin again with every moment. Or, rather, atheism, which is a choice of the mind, never penetrates to the deepest levels of the human heart. "To be at peace with one's dead" is the first form assumed by the desire to be at peace with God.

Between Stendhal and Mérimée there was not the distance that separated Elpenor from Ulysses. If Mérimée was Ulysses, Stendhal was at least Achilles. That is why one shouldn't attach too much importance to this latter Elpenor. It forms the opening in a minor key of a funeral speech in which there are many joyful notes and tender melodies. "Pagan funeral," says Mérimée. It was not for him to sing hymns.

Sautelet would be more like Elpenor than Beyle, since Elpenor there was. One sometimes comes across his name when exploring the nineteenth century. It is a charming, light-hearted name; what despairing spirit lurked behind it? In *La Vie de Henry Brulard* Stendhal says, "M. Sautelet, the liberal bookseller, blew out his brains in about 1829 through a mixture of vanity, love and debts. He was a director of the newspaper *Le National* and an associate of the honest, patriotic and foolish Paulin, who was still a bookseller in 1836." Armand Carrel, in June 1830, devoted an article to Sautelet entitled "Une Mort Volontaire." "This weak but good young man . . ." he wrote. Sainte-Beuve, finally, speaks of "Sautelet's laughing and bald young head"—which, in one line, gives an excellent portrait of a desperate man. Sautelet admired *Obermann*;* he proclaimed himself a follower of Sénancour, which was very romantic but rather silly, to my way of thinking. "Restless, melancholy and ardent, he hovered between action and contemplation," says Sainte-Beuve, who quotes the following passage from one of his letters: "One can hardly lead a double life of action and contemplation. . . . I should like to blow my brains out, to put an end to my doubts. If, in a year or two, life doesn't seem clearer to me, I shall put an end to it.

---

* A once famous but now forgotten novel by the nineteenth-century author Sénancour.—Tr.

I shall carry out the idea I had in my *Werther de la vérité* [a work he was planning]. Perhaps this would be madness; perhaps it would be a great action. . . ." All this is very sad, no doubt, and very touching, but rather silly. When you come down to it, Stendhal, as always, summed up Sautelet's case correctly. Vanity played a large part in this stoical and philosophical suicide. Let us be generous and say pride. But this is hardly any more respectable. Victor Cousin's prudence is unpleasant. These fashionable philosophers, who earn renown by bringing other philosophers within reach of the public, by writing a little on politics, literature, the fine arts or famous women, are not, I suspect, very reliable men. They think too much of their careers and the opinions of their disciples.

We are better informed on Victor Jacquemont than on Sautelet. He left behind him two volumes of letters. MM. Geoffroy Saint-Hilaire and Cambessèdes in 1835 published a six-volume *Journal complet de V. Jacquemont, avec les descriptions zoologiques et botaniques,* in which they assembled all the material the author had collected for a great work. Jacquemont also gave his name to a genus of subshrubs belonging to the family of Convolvulaceae, including several species growing at the Cape of Good Hope, which are known as jacquemontias.

A great botanist, the pride of the Paris Museum of Natural History, Jacquemont emerges as a sort of Byron of the sciences, but with a more naïve and honest genius. He roamed the earth collecting flowers in order to forget an unhappy love affair. He was a friend of Lafayette, Dumont d'Urville, Stendhal, Mérimée and the Baron de Mareste, the latter a strange and sarcastic character, a man of the eighteenth century strayed into the nineteenth, to whom we shall return later.

On August 26, 1828, at the age of twenty-seven, Jacquemont set sail for India, where he was to die four years later. He left his parents, so the Goncourt brothers report in their

Journal, "with as lighthearted a farewell as if he were going to St.-Cloud." This simplicity is sublime. The previous year, through his charm, gentleness of manner, earnestness and liking for understatement, he had won the hearts of the English aristocracy in London, by no means the least of his exploits and one that earned him undreamed-of letters of introduction to all sorts of governors and rajahs. In India he behaved like a modest hero. We see him striding over the Himalayas with a bamboo cane and a hammer in his hand, sounding the rocks and exploring the layers, living on boiled rice and leathery goat's meat, sleeping in a tent. In Tibet, by means of a vehement speech and the sight of a group of ruffians he had taken for company, he terrified a Chinese officer who was inimical to botany. It was on the peaks of Kedar Kanta, at a height of ten thousand feet, that he felt the first attacks of the liver infection which was to kill him. This delightful young man, this great scholar, this philosopher whom the Indian people elected to be their judge and arbiter wherever he went, to whom maharajahs offered palaces, and whose sole fortune was an allowance of six thousand francs granted him by the museum, was also an excellent writer. His letters are admirable, both for their sensibility and for their style; the notes in his *Journal* inspire the deepest regret. Had he not died at the age of thirty-one, he would have been another Buffon.

Here is a sketch of Jacquemont by Mérimée to which there is nothing to add:

> His method of pleasing consisted in making no attempt to disguise his thoughts or feelings, in being completely natural. Few people fail to respond to such frankness when it is accompanied by an original mind and a sound education. I have sometimes heard him accused of a taste for paradox. In my opinion, this was certainly not one of his faults. On the contrary, in every argument in which

he took part he was, or believed himself to be, on the side of truth; but he often gave his thoughts an odd twist, which might have led those who pay more heed to form than to content to misconstrue them. The charm of his wit lay precisely in its being neither contrived nor affected. I should add that the remarkably pleasant timbre of his voice perhaps contributed not a little to his success as a conversationalist. I have never heard a more naturally musical voice. Hearing him talk reminded me of these lines of Shakespeare:

> Oh! it came on my ears like the sweet south*
> That breathes upon a bank of violets.

I don't propose to overlook his faults. Foolishness—above all stupidity—irritated him strangely. He couldn't stand it and would fly into a rage. Beyle, who, although himself very intolerant in this respect, nevertheless preserved a certain tact, reproached him for getting seriously worked up over people who had the misfortune to be stupid. "Do you imagine," he added, "that they do it on purpose?" "I have no idea," replied Jacquemont savagely.

It is not hard to imagine the quality of the friendship which bound Stendhal to his young friends Jacquemont and Mérimée. He was eighteen years older than the first and twenty years older than the second. From the point of view of their friendship it was a stroke of luck that his fame bore no relation to his genius. However self-possessed, however conscious Mérimée was of his own superiority, too great a renown on Stendhal's part would have brought a hint of constraint into their relationship. Instead of this, Mérimée's admiration al-

---

* The error here—"south" for "sound"—is Mérimée's. He translated Shakespeare's "sweet sound" as *doux vent du Midi*."—Tr.

ways remained greater than his friend's reputation. Stendhal must have doted on Jacquemont, who had all the right qualities to please him—frankness, that love of truth which gave his remarks the strange appeal of raw materials, and finally the enterprising and beguiling ways of a slightly wayward man. This vitality, this desire for success and this charm are often the attributes of scoundrels. With a sort of angel like Jacquemont, it must have cast a spell to which Mérimée, who so loved ardent spirits, responded as eagerly as Stendhal. For me, Jacquemont had all the characteristics of Lucien Leuwen; he was a Stendhalian hero. Plainly, with him we are very far from the good Elpenor.

Beyle, original in all he did, which is a true merit in this age of faded manners, prided himself on his liberalism but was at heart a thorough aristocrat. He could never suffer fools; he cherished a furious hatred for the people who bored him, and, all his life, he never learned how to distinguish clearly a malicious man from a tiresome one.

FADED MANNERS are still manners, and nothing is so stimulating as these pallid manners. *H.B.* was published in 1850; however faded they were, the manners were still perfectly visible. Everyone had the attitudes of his class, which provided a fairly clear picture of society. The bourgeoisie defended the throne, the altar, the army and their private incomes. The dancers at the Opéra were concierges' daughters.

An "original" is merely a sensible man who, out of a concern for justice, follows the course opposite to the manners of his time so as to prevent the balance from swinging too far to one side. He sees the absurdity and transience of fashions too clearly not to make fun of them; he judges and behaves according to his natural simplicity, intensified by a spirit of contradiction. In fact, he follows the golden mean, leaning toward conservatism when the fashion is revolution, and vice versa. A census of original men throughout the centuries would show them to be all alike. But originality has its blessed and its accursed periods. In 1830 it was a joy to be original in the face of Comte Molé, Guizot, Villemain and the rest, in a bourgeois, implacable France which presented her opinions to the world in alternate bouts of intelligence and stupidity. In 1958, in an anarchistic France where there are no manners, or mores, left at all, it is a great misfortune; one is driven to the right, one aspires to restore these manners to their rightful place, and so on. You will scarcely find an original man in Paris today. The immensity of the task discourages them. Perhaps they are also afraid, for societies without manners are pitiless toward them. I have seen a few originals in Moscow and New York, where there are still manners; they are quite happy and at peace with themselves, more or less as an original could be a hundred years ago in Paris.

The characteristic of the original is to defend liberty. This is very pleasant under a despotic government. When abuse of liberty is the common rule, it becomes an act of heroism. Stendhal with his revolutionary ideas and his jokes would pass in 1958 for an abominable reactionary, an upholder of the moral order, a chauvinist—in short, a back number.

To pride oneself on liberalism and be at heart a thorough aristocrat is a good definition of the artist. Intelligence and good taste (above all when this is carried to a sublime degree, as with Stendhal) condemn you to the aristocracy; reason and generosity condemn you to liberalism. This division of the heart could make great kings.

Stendhal's furious hatred for those who bored him was the normal reaction of a hard-working writer who despairingly sees his precious time, which he takes off from work only to pursue pleasure or passion, being uselessly dissipated. There are forceful passages on this feeling in Montherlant's *Carnets*. These include an excellent phrase, "the tragedies of politeness," which aptly expresses the horror of the time it causes one to waste. "How can we make someone 'nice' understand that the four hours we are to spend dining and talking at his house could be far better employed by us? . . . How are we to make him understand that true kindness toward us would be best expressed by not inviting us? . . . Friendship corrupts itself when it does not willingly take a vacation. . . ." And so on. Were I to let myself go, I could be as inexhaustible as Stendhal and Montherlant on this subject. But there is no call for me to describe again what has already been so well described. Montherlant is a master on boredom in society. No one has better outlined its causes, its repercussions, its effects; no one has drawn a more telling philosophy or moral from it; no one has given better or more brutal recipes for dispelling it. He calls the bore a "life eater." I had already read the term "time eater" somewhere. The bore browses on your time, that is to say on your life; therefore it is all just as if he were a really malicious man of the worst possible kind.

He professed to a deep contempt for the French character and would eloquently point out all the faults of which our great nation is no doubt wrongly accused—irresponsibility, thoughtlessness, inconsistency in both words and deeds. At heart he had these same faults to a high degree and, to mention thoughtlessness alone, he wrote a letter in code one day to M. de Broglie, the Minister of Foreign Affairs, and enclosed the code in the same envelope.

*F*EW AUTHORS have written as stirring passages on the French character as the opening pages of *La Chartreuse de Parme*. They hymn the French character in 1796. Through the two wars of 1914 and 1939 we have learned that twenty-five years are enough to turn an intrepid people into cowards. The society of Louis Philippe, so remarkable in so many respects, was plainly less interesting that the society of the Revolution, in which everything was done by young and poor men. One can understand how Stendhal, who had had the good fortune to witness "miracles of bravery and genius," despised the Bourbons, the Orléans, their bankers and their police. For several years Napoleon's companions had believed that France was the future of the world. Given such a belief, patriotism is intoxicating. Happy are they who live through such periods, when a nation covers its sons with glory! In 1815 the men who, ever since Valmy and Jemmapes, had been giving birth to the future became ex-servicemen, and the "Empire style," that style of the new age, became a thing of the past.

Since France thereafter filled him with horror, Beyle fled to Italy, where he consoled himself for no longer roaming the world with Napoleon Bonaparte by observing the passions of eager hearts. The lines in which he depicts the French character are accurate, merciless and famous: "In France, poverty is a source of ridicule; vanity is the national passion of France; one sees received in the best of society people with futile honor, without genuine honor, whereas the contrary is impossible . . ." and so on. One can read a hundred judgments of this kind in his works. They express the views of an ex-serviceman, but a highly perceptive one. They annoyed Sainte-Beuve, who never went to war and who was, on his own admission, a coward. I have known ex-servicemen from the 1914 war, genuinely brave men, who in turn began in about 1930 to develop a horror of the country for which they would have laid down their lives fifteen years before. I wonder if the Germans, the Russians or the English know these paroxysms of exaltation and disgust, which are clearly two sides of the same passion. So these are the people for whom I was ready to die, one says to oneself fifteen years after. Thus do great love affairs end.

Stendhal's literary friends, particularly Mérimée, were all twenty years younger than he. In spite of his genius, which was capable of bridging every gap, in spite of his conviction that one must bestride the various periods of one's life as if they were stages along a road, without becoming more attached to one than to another, in spite of his cult of happiness *now*, this survivor of the wars of the Empire, this retired soldier amidst the children of the century stood out from the rest. He had actually lived through what seemed to them a fabulous, mythological epic, and as a man come from the eighteenth century, that is to say from the back of beyond, the product of a different, almost incomprehensible civilization. A reader of Voltaire, a young Jacobin, a Bonapartist in the Empire style, Stendhal had nothing in common with the sensibility of the Romantics. When one compares Musset to Mérimée, one measures his influence on the latter. Stendhal was nostalgic for glory, but he had known it for twenty-five years. These twenty-five years of apprenticeship, during which he was too busy to write as a professional man of letters, greatly enlarged his heart. The France of the Congress of Vienna, Talleyrand and the Restoration could not fill it. All Napoleon's companions had lived through the same tragedy as their master. Each of them had known his St. Helena, down to the abject Capitaine Giroudeau of Balzac's *Illusions perdues*. Clemenceau, in 1925, despaired of the France he himself had led to victory.

There are several Frances. The France of the salons, of public life in peacetime, which sets the form and dictates the fashion, is delightful and hateful; it has hardly altered since Louis XIV. One is astonished to find it identical down the centuries in the descriptions of good authors—Saint-Simon, Marivaux, Louvet, Balzac, Victor Hugo, Proust. Same words, same cattiness, same luxury, same habits. I sometimes go out into "society" in Paris with the feelings of a historian or an archaeologist. What I see and hear there takes me back one or two hundred years. I reflect that this survival of former times, of the old civilization, into our modern age is an astonishing and doubtless precious thing, like a piece of period furniture or a historic house, and that its charm and edification must be savored to the last drop. This "society" is degraded, certainly; it hasn't the grand style it had in 1700 or even in 1840, or even in 1910; between this world and the court of Louis XV there is as great a difference as between a Boulle cupboard encrusted with gold and tortoise shell and a mid-Victorian mahogany commode. But the tradition has been upheld, in spite of the revolutions of 1789, 1830 and 1848, the Commune and the advent in 1945 of the two hydrocephalic eagles of Russia and America.

The poilus of the Great War were a second edition of the veterans of the Empire. From such books as the *Cahiers du Capitaine Coignet,* countless descriptions of imperial campaigns, Raffet's lithographs and similar material, combined with the memories of my father, a veteran of the 1914-18 war, I have discovered a striking resemblance between these two armies with a hundred years between them. The emotions that inspired their bravery and cheerfulness were the same. I may say that, in my own way, I have known the "Empire style," which, moreover, is tending to disappear the more the survivors of World War I disappear or subside into old age. It isn't hard to imagine Stendhal's fellow feelings for the brave soldiers of Jena and Wagram. I myself can picture him very well, delightedly listening to Balzac's Goguelat, "talking Napoleon" in his barn. I am certain that in Paris he more than once had one of those wonderful encounters with a veteran at some street corner, running unexpectedly into one of General Éblé's pontoniers or a survivor of Champaubert whose acquaintance he had made fifteen years earlier between two volleys of cannon fire. I was five, or possibly six, when one day with eyes popping I saw my father, a dentist of normally bourgeois habits and rather a lofty manner toward those he called his "inferiors," hugging a taxi driver who had driven the two of us somewhere or other. The taxi driver kept excitedly repeating, *"Mon lieutenant! Mon lieutenant!"* My father, too, was deeply moved. This scene has remained engraved in my memory. At the time, I felt there was something mysterious and epic about it. What an adventure the war must have been, to have swept aside the social barriers toward the maintenance of which my father was sensitive to the point of punctiliousness! Stendhal, in frock coat and beaver hat, treading the streets of Paris with the light step of a rather portly man, must have had wonderful talks with cabdrivers and ex-sergeants filling their leisure hours by seasoning pipes at the Palais-Royal. The spirit of the Revolution and the Empire no doubt was revived intact and these memories must have given intense pleasure to Beyle, so bored by the insipid good manners of the Restoration nobility.

When one has lived with heroes who have jovially carved out an empire vaster than Alexander's, when one has been a hero oneself out of an infectious desire to emulate the others, and when the tide of history has cast you into the middle of a society absorbed by idiotic poses and farm rents, one some-times feels sad and empty at heart. This sadness and emptiness are increased by the sight of former heroes now dismissed and turned sullen, jobless and resentful, dragging their boots along the pavements. Despite a few happy encounters or a talk led by bugle calls about the charge at Wagram, what a grim gen-eral picture—a France that had lapsed into the futilities and in-justices of the doddering *ancien régime,* with all its energies put toward anticipated retirement, and over all this the White Terror* and the *milliard des émigrés!*† Stendhal's road, which led from the Berezina to the Faubourg St.-Germain, was the road of a soul into exile.

The affair of the coded letter with the code forwarded in the same envelope to M. de Broglie, whatever Mérimée felt about it, reveals something other than thoughtlessness. If it wasn't a joke on Beyle's part, it seems to me that a psy-chiatrist might well discover in it an unconscious contempt for the government of Louis Philippe. The interests of that par-

---

* The revenge taken by the refugees from the Revolution after the Res-toration of 1815.—Tr.
† On their return to France, the émigrés extorted from the government an indemnity of a billion gold francs which was paid for by the taxpayers. —Tr.

ticular France must have seemed very paltry to a man who had known the immense ones of the great France of Napoleon. The game was no longer worth the candle. Certainly, Beyle was too honest a functionary to entertain such thoughts and to apply them, but the code in the letter nonetheless constitutes a fine Freudian slip.

4

Throughout his life he was dominated by his imagination, and everything he did was done abruptly and enthusiastically. Yet he prided himself on always acting solely according to the laws of reason. "One must be guided in everything by Lo-gic," he used to say, leaving a pause between the first and second syllables of the word; but he seethed with impatience when the logic of others was not the same as his own. Besides, he scarcely ever argued. Those who didn't know him attributed to an excessive pride what was probably merely respect for other people's convictions. "You are a cat, I am a rat," he used to say, by way of concluding the argument.

SUDDEN ACTIONS provoked by enthusiasm are the most delightful of all; they are the luxury of men of sensibility who know themselves for what they are, of honest hearts who rely on their natural honesty. One never repents of such actions, even if they lead to disastrous consequences, so keen is the happiness one gets from deciding to take them. They have the charm of the unforeseen; the soul leans out of the window and discovers a new landscape. Finally, the pleasure of telling oneself that one is not a man to hesitate before a potential gratification or a good deed, that one can, on occasion, make up one's mind in a flash, is infinitely stimulating. I can understand how Stendhal succumbed to it all his life. The imagination rides out ahead like a horseman, barely glances at the terrain to be reconnoitered, finds it the most beautiful in the world and goes into battle singlehanded, without waiting

27

for the main body of the army. By and large, the outcome of these engagements matters little, whether one emerges from them victorious or vanquished, so great is the pleasure of throwing oneself into them. I have committed two kinds of folly in my life: the considered and the impulsive. Those in the first category leave me only a bad taste; they were boring, like sensible actions, duly thought out and coldly performed. The others, being in line with my character, at least amused me. Besides, they have always proved of less consequence, for I was less persistent about them.

The spirit of contradiction is a strange passion which feeds on any kind of nourishment, and one begins by practicing it against oneself. Setting up a cult of reason and logic was the way in which Beyle resisted his enthusiasms and rash impulses. It seemed to him sublime to be cold, because he was boiling over. His work is full of such contradictions. What could be more contradictory than the plots and characters of *Le Rouge et le Noir* or *La Chartreuse de Parme* on the one hand and the style of these novels on the other? This fundamental disparity has a great deal to do with their prodigious appeal.

I am familiar with the workings and effects of the spirit of contradiction, since I am afflicted by it myself as much as anyone can be, but I have never completely extracted a philosophy from it. Is it an exaggerated and provocative form of the sense of justice, which by implication impels one to side with the minority, to take one's stand under the banner of the weakest, in order thereby to compensate for its weakness, in order to redress to some degree the dissymmetry of the world? Is it an innate disposition, or a sentiment acquired during childhood in the wake of petty revolts and through the conviction that one is not at all of the same nature as those who surround one? I remember that when I was seven or eight I already vaguely but wholeheartedly detested the way of living, ideas, narrow principles, clichés and cautious and commonplace conformity of the petty-bourgeois world in which I lived. With much rancor and bitterness I was accused of wanting to "attract attention," to "assert myself," to "make myself interesting" and so on. But I couldn't do otherwise. I was impelled by some indefinable force. These accusations of originality at all costs pursued me very late into life—up to the age of twenty-four or -five at least—and, when it became necessary to earn my living, brought me many rebuffs. The character, the way of life, even the language of the people in whose company I worked filled me with a curious aversion which impelled me to adopt contrary attitudes. These in no sense reflected my true nature; other people's hypocrisy drove me to excesses of frankness, their feigned humility to excesses of pride. Because of this, I was dismissed from many jobs and sometimes reduced to financial straits. Perhaps the spirit of contradiction is the unfortunate attribute of those who have only belatedly discovered the inner world to which they belong. For myself, I glimpsed this for the first time when I was fourteen, reading Anatole France in secret; and because of this, despite his faults, I have retained a slight affection for him. He said what I was thinking, and the opposite of what my family was saying. It was not until after I had turned twenty that I read a book by Stendhal. My amazement knew no bounds. At last I had found my native land! I was a different person after reading this book. Stendhal was for me a bridge, thanks to which I could quit a world to which I never returned, crossing over into another whose outlook and philosophy I adopted then and there, without any reservations.

One must seek in Grenoble for the origins of the spirit of contradiction in Stendhal. "I noticed with my sister Pauline, who shared my views," he writes in *Brulard*, "that the conversation during the best moment of the day, while taking coffee, always consisted of whining. They whined about everything." Petty provincial society at the end of the *ancien régime* must have been frightful. But at ten, Stendhal had the luck to see the Revolution decapitate the people who had exasperated him, or at least their like. At eighteen, a sublieutenant of dragoons in the army in Italy, one can understand why he was mad about the Republic, which had overthrown the old world he had known in its most repellent form—narrowminded ecclesiastics, a stupid squirearchy, a paternalistic and futile nobility and all those idiotic elders and betters who make childhood such a detestable age. What joy to be eighteen in 1801! There was not one old man in the government, and those who weren't young were at least intelligent. Everything was redolent of glory and grandeur. There were still ten years of intoxication ahead. It is regrettable that no young man of that time ever wrote an account of his sentimental education. All we possess is Stendhal's brief and fragmentary *Journal*. No doubt, happiness and power are hardly conducive to literature. Sentimental educations are for hearts that bleed or fret from boredom.

At forty, under the Restoration, Stendhal found himself plunged back into the society of his childhood, made worse by old age and struggling to destroy the last vestiges of what had been the enchantment of his young manhood. "Social despair" has never been seriously studied. This sort of despair, in various degrees, was felt by the majority of the veterans of the Grande Armée, just as today it is felt by those who cannot adapt themselves to a shrunken and shivering nation. It is one of the extreme forms of patriotism, "that horrible disease," as Montherlant calls it, "but no more so than any other love." I don't think Stendhal gave much evidence of his spirit of contradiction between 1801 and 1815, for Bonaparte offered him marvels which certainly thrilled him and he infinitely relished the actions of that "great soul," as he calls him several times in his *Vie de Napoléon*. But he must have recovered it intact after Waterloo, when he had to begin a whole new life and when he remembered that he was a writer of genius.

An author's age is to be reckoned in terms of his work or fame. We see young authors of fifty and old authors of thirty. Stendhal remained a "young author" for a long time. (One can measure this clearly from the tone of the *Lundi* devoted to him by Sainte-Beuve. For all that Stendhal was dead, the celebrated critic twenty years his junior still treated him with a friendly condescension which posterity has made comic. What can it have been like in his lifetime?) But he never had the respectful manners, the shyness and tact of a beginner. He behaved like a man fully aware of his genius, brushing aside accepted ideas, making savage fun of things, brusquely interrupting the talkers and talking hugely himself. One overlooks everything from a famous man, from an old man of thirty, even if he has no true merit. Everything is a sin from a fellow who is not recognized by the press, even if he has the most dazzling gifts. I imagine that Stendhal talked with the same fire and zest that he put into his writing. It is a fascinating thing to compose a book when one doesn't know it beforehand, when one discovers it as one goes along and thereby discovers oneself. Stendhal, like all good authors, must have often snared ideas as he talked. This hardly promotes silence, or even discretion. No evening out is wasted if one can say to oneself on returning home, "I wasn't bored; I talked the whole time. And I always find something to learn from what I say."

What Mérimée reports of Stendhal is typical of the superior man, very sure of his ideas because he has tested them over a long period. Refusal to argue is the sign of a writer who considers that he has put the essence of his thought into his books —people need only refer to them if they want to know what it is. Why tire oneself out spouting rhetoric when one has already written the same thing so clearly and definitively? The "respect for the convictions of others" seems to me a fool-hardy assertion, the sort of silly remark one finds in panegyrics or obituaries, as out of place in this text as a thoughtless *gruppetto* in a piece of music. Genius doesn't go in for such considerations; it cares only for the truth, of which it believes itself to be the touchstone. Here is a passage from *Brulard* which to some extent gives the lie to Mérimée's mildness: "I may say that the approval of people whom I regard as weak is utterly indifferent to me. As far as I am concerned they are mad, and I clearly see that they don't understand the problem." Stendhal was not mistaken as to the convictions of those to whom he talked. His silence no more signified pride than it did respect; he simply expressed the conviction that one has no chance of bringing home the truth to someone who is defend-ing error, and that no purpose is served by wearing oneself out at it. Confucius, five hundred years, and Chuang-tzu, three hundred years before Christ, used to say, "After forty, faults are incorrigible," and "Light does not spring from argument." More recently, Léon-Paul Fargue told me something I have never forgotten: "One cannot argue unless one is in agree-ment. On points of detail, if that!" As for other people's logic, it isn't surprising that Stendhal detested it if it disagreed with his own. His was the good one.

I have long brooded over the formula, "You are a cat, I am a rat," which is mysterious and poetic.* Insolent, too, for

---

* Here is another saying of Léon-Paul Fargue's which fits admirably into this context:

  I see La Fontaine wandering like a friendly and compact vole, like a field mouse which slips into the farms, finding there a corner under the fond eyes of the peasants, waxes fat, dreams for a few days or weeks and then sets out again for the cornfields. Thus La Fontaine spent months with Fouquet, years with Mme. de la Sab-lière and, after her, moved on somewhere else with his mouse's tread, making little sound on the pavements of Paris, but knowing where he was going.

Stendhal prefers the rat, that savage little beast, to the cat, a large domestic animal entrusted with the maintenance of order to the benefit of man. The weak, abject rat—pursued by all, surrounded by traps, snares and arsenic, stealing its food, leading a life full of risk and danger, sheltering in drains, carrying the plague—is the most wretched creature in the world. To liken oneself to a rat is one of those keen pleasures of humility courted by truly proud spirits. A rat would never allow itself to face up to a cat; it would be caught and devoured in a flash. Stendhal, whatever Mérimée says, was clearly using this ironic way out to cover up his pride. When a superior man says something to a fool which means, "You are too strong for me," he is having a bit of fun.

In 1813, Beyle was the involuntary witness of the rout of a whole brigade unexpectedly charged by five hundred Cossacks. Beyle saw about two thousand men turn and run, including five generals, recognizable by their frogged hats. He ran like the rest, but clumsily, having only one foot shod and carrying the other boot in his hand. In the whole of this French corps, there were only two heroes who faced up to the Cossacks: a guardsman called Menneval and a conscript who, trying to fire on the Cossacks, killed the guardsman's horse. Beyle was charged with the task of describing this panic to the Emperor, who listened to him with concentrated fury, the while he kept turning one of those iron contraptions which serve to fix the shutters. A search was made for the guardsman, in order to give him a medal, but he hid himself and at first denied having had anything to do with the affair, convinced that nothing is so bad as to attract attention during a rout. He thought they wanted to have him shot.

THIS PARAGRAPH makes an absorbing tale on several accounts. To begin with, there is a splendid description of a military scene from which nothing is missing: the panic, the five frogged hats, the central character hopping along in flight clutching one boot in his hand, and the two heroes—the veteran and the recruit. The date of 1813 casts a wan and tragic light on this picture. In sixteen lines of prose, Mérimée portrays the whole Grande Armée, from the conscript to the

Emperor, via the generals; he also provides first-class testimony as to the morals and sensibility of the period. The behavior of the guardsman Menneval offers a closer insight than any sociological work into the ideas, principles, ways of being, instinctive reactions, emotions and conception of honor which men had in France at the beginning of the nineteenth century. I must confess that I find this guardsman Menneval delightful. What bravery! What modesty! What an exact sense of collective responsibility! This man, who had nothing for which to blame himself, who had done his duty, felt dishonored by his brigade and, prudently, thought only of taking shelter behind anonymous cowardice. Say after that that the Frenchman is an individualist! He has become one, perhaps because he has been taught that nothing is so glorious as winning quiz contests, owning a hideous suburban house which "reflects his personality," and so on; but he wasn't one in Menneval's time. That the brave guardsman was afraid of being shot as a reward for his courageous action shows his wisdom and respect for a society which didn't trifle with sound principles.

I like the Emperor's "concentrated fury" quite as much as Menneval's sensible misgivings. The flight of one of his own brigades wounded him personally, just as a father might consider himself dishonored by a cowardly act on the part of his son. It is a long time since we have witnessed such righteous anger on the part of a general or a minister. It has again become the fashion today, as it was under the Restoration, to refer to Napoleon as an ogre, but even were that great soul the monster he is made out to be, the fact still remains that this concentrated fury of 1813, faithfully transmitted by Beyle to Mérimée and by the latter to us, not forgetting the detail of the iron contraption which served to fix the shutters, proves a love which one would have to attain oneself before venturing to cast the first stone. The last reaction of a French statesman toward the cravenness of his compatriots which history has recorded is that of M. Daladier returning from Munich in September 1938 and being astonished to find that the Parisian crowd that had come to meet him, far from booing him, gave him a deafening ovation. *"Quels cons!"* he sighed to St. John Perse, seated beside him in the triumphal car. I know one must not belittle M. Daladier, of whom the same St. John Perse said to me (in October 1956) that he hadn't cut too bad a figure at Munich and had even displayed a sort of irascible patriotism; I know one should see discouragement rather than contempt in his exclamation; but we are still far from the concentrated fury of the Emperor, and the two attitudes set the tone of the two epochs, alas.

Finally, the heroic Menneval's fear teaches us that bravery is a fashion, an emotion as artificially imposed as the cut of one's clothes. The fact that one might be afraid incurred the Emperor's sovereign displeasure; so one was brave, to please him—and to better oneself. Bravery was "the thing." In this way nations from time to time have the luck to be ruled by superior men of common sense, who imbue the uncertain minds and hearts of the people with noble desires. Between 1940 and 1944 bad soldiers trembled before General de Gaulle, that great man, who loved them but would never have hesitated to have them shot. In the same way, they had trembled before Clemenceau. But what respect would they have felt for poor Gamelin and his emulators? Under Napoleon, at least up to 1805, one had to be either very intelligent or very brave to achieve a high position, for one was constantly being judged by a great soul.

As a pendant to the attitude of the guardsman Menneval, convinced that nothing is so bad as to attract attention during a rout, I shall take the liberty of quoting a dispatch published in the newspaper *L'Éclaireur de Nice* in September 1940: "X, a first-class gunner, took part in the glorious retreat of over four hundred kilometers which has enabled the Seventh Army victoriously to resist all the assaults of the enemy; has always courageously and cheerfully done his duty. *Has not known defeat.* This mention brings with it the award of the Croix de Guerre with bronze star." Isn't everything about this dispatch staggering? I am not denying that the gunner X was a courageous and cheerful fellow, but what *can* he have known in 1940 if he didn't know defeat? Plainly, in 1940 it wasn't so bad as in 1813 to attract attention during a rout. (And what a rout! There were far more than two thousand men and five frogged hats!)

Stendhal hopping along clutching one of his boots makes a pleasant picture. At least that is how he described himself in his story to Mérimée, who passed it on to us with his usual fidelity, acute ear and infallible feeling for the vital detail. Some will perhaps see in this hobbling flight agitation, confusion, a mind smitten with stupor, a share in the general panic. For myself, I see in it the very opposite: complete self-possession, a countenance superior to the circumstances, a desire to add a subtle note of irony and ridicule to a terrible scene, as if to devaluate it. There was nothing to prevent Stendhal from pulling on his boot and running as fast as the rest of the brigade. I am willing to bet that, if he didn't do so, it was out of pure modesty, pure seemliness, a sort of self-respect in the midst of so many men who had suddenly lost all self-respect. To hop along with one boot in one's hand is certainly not a romantic, lyrical way to behave, but in certain instances it takes on the value of a manifesto. Stendhal hopping on one leg, stopping every now and then to cast a curious and disapproving eye on the fleeing men pushing and shouting as they shot past him like arrows; Stendhal wallowing in his spirit of contradiction; Stendhal glancing to right and left with a false air of astonishment; Stendhal, finally, quite unperturbed by the thought of being killed by a spear thrust from one of the ferocious Cossacks, provides a fine picture of the intrepid philosopher who refuses to let himself be caught up in the terrors of the vulgar mob.

That Stendhal was later charged with describing this panic to the Emperor, instead of one of the five frogged hats who had played such an active part in it, proves that destiny doesn't choose badly those to whom she wishes to offer sensations.

6

Beyle was more eloquent about love than about war. I have never seen him other than in love or believing himself to be so; but he had had two great love-passions (to use one of his own expressions) of which he never managed to cure himself.
One, the earliest in date, I think, was inspired by Mme. C——, then at the height of her dazzling beauty. He counted many powerful men among his rivals, including Caulaincourt, a general much in favor, who one day took advantage of his position to force Beyle to yield him his place in the lady's favors.

That same evening, Beyle found a means to impart to him a little fable of his own composition, in which he allegorically challenged him to a duel. I don't know if the fable was understood, but its moral was not accepted, and Beyle received a severe reprimand from his relative and protector, M. Daru. He nonetheless continued to press his suit.

*H*AVING READ Balzac, not in the way that Fabre studied insects (for he put much fantasy and humor into this) but like the most arid of biologists examining bacteria under a microscope, P——, a member of the Université de France, claims to have found in *La Comédie humaine* six Vautrins who differ from each other in some minute but revealing detail. These contradictory details are obviously not of the slightest importance.* They are the oversights of a mighty genius caught

---

* God—God Himself—does not proceed otherwise; his creatures are never the same two days running. A man may be chaste on Monday and lecherous on Tuesday, mean on Saturday and prodigal on Sunday.

up in a whirlwind, in a masked ball of the imagination for which the members of the university have no ticket of admission. They stand at the ballroom door and criticize the costumes of the guests. Inside there are prodigious passions, dazzling conversation and divine music, of which they catch only a confused jumble of sounds. Little do they care, in any case; they are interested only in the costumes.

It is not necessary to look for costumes, that is to say biography, in this book. Stendhal won't suffer for it, in any case. He has had more biographers (beginning with himself) than anyone else and his biographers are all models of piety, scrupulousness and pedantry. We even know the walks he went on, and they dispute over stray quarters of an hour. Such meticulousness is futile. The ideal history would no doubt be a mirror of life, its complete record; but in that case, how it would encumber the world! The more details it accumulates, the less interest it offers, for erudition is the enemy of meditation. History is interesting only for the moral or philosophy one can draw from it. If it confines itself to amassing as many events as possible without any spirit of synthesis, it merely becomes second-rate journalism applied to the past.

The few disorderly and scrappy memories that Mérimée troubled to record about Stendhal, which doubtless contain errors that horrify the professional Stendhalians and which M. Martineau* accuses of having in every instance been contrived "with a view to the effect they would produce," seem to me more precious than the fat volumes full of ascertained facts that have appeared over the past fifty years, for they come from a man who not only lived in close contact with his subject (which could mean little) but also, and more particularly, knew what was insignificant and what was not.

Mme. C—— is the Comtesse Curial, a woman with whom

---

* The most famous of Stendhal's biographers.—TR.

one feels in love even from this distance. She consoled Beyle for the horrible Métilde; thus she wasn't his first but his second love-passion. He had come on her unawares, barefooted, in the country, in 1814. The memory of those charming little feet coiled itself round his heart for ten years; he became her lover only in 1824. There still exists an anonymous terracotta bust, as graceful as a work by Houdon, depicting the Comtesse Curial in the full flower of her youth: she has well-defined eyebrows, the strong neck of a sensual woman, a pensive air and tender lips. Her pleated Empire dress, with its round collar, and her simple coiffure vaguely in the antique style make her very desirable. Her rather protruding but exquisite nose, her little rounded forehead, are still those of a child, as are her cheeks with their downy and indefinite contours. The carriage of her head is that of a young girl of good family, doubtless strictly brought up and pure, but open to the charms of wantonness. One can sense behind all this a very seductive blend of goodness and compliance. I forgot to mention the eyes, large, well shaped, rather grave and empty—the most beautiful one could wish to see.

Appearances deceive only those who mistrust them or incurable fools. Mme. Curial's appearance conforms with her character. Both her face and her soul have the same sweetness and tenderness, the same delicious softness. I can understand how, for love of this ravishing creature, a man could go so far as to provoke a duel with General Caulaincourt, who was almost as powerful as the Emperor. To get a true idea of Beyle's audacity, one has to imagine a little clerk in the commissariat of the Wehrmacht sending a challenge to his rival Goering in 1938. But I find it hard to picture this kind of courage in a German. Besides, the Germany of 1938 was gloomy and repellant. It bears no possible resemblance to the France of Napoleon, which was healthy, had inherited almost all the gaiety and tolerance of the *ancien régime* and, finally, was the only country in Europe where there was any enlightenment. A reprimand from M. Daru and the risk of jeopardizing his career counted for little in Beyle's eyes compared with possession of Mme. Curial. A great example of a man who never deceived himself over the true value of things, and for whom happiness came before vanity. To provoke General Caulaincourt by imparting a little fable to him fires one with admiration for its elegance. This is straight out of *Faublas*,* and it will be found again in Stendhal's novels.

---

* A famous eighteenth-century novel, *Adventures du Chevalier de Faublas*, by Louvet de Couvrai.—Tr.

To me, Beyle always seemed convinced of the idea, widely held under the Empire, that a woman can always be taken by storm and that it is every man's duty to attempt this.

"Have her; it is first and foremost what you owe her," *he used to tell me whenever I talked to him of a woman with whom I was in love.*

Sᴛᴇɴᴅʜᴀʟ's *Journal* contains a number of gross obscenities. These include a concise description of the ways of Lesbians and a recipe for raping a woman. Apart from the pleasure of pinning down a truth, one can feel the kind of satisfaction Beyle got from writing these. It is always foolish to go in for psychoanalysis or psychology. Still, one can't dispense with it here. In all the indecent or crude passages in the *Journal*, the *Souvenirs d'égotisme* or *Brulard*, I believe that Beyle was as much revenging himself on his childhood in Grenoble as thumbing his nose at his past as a shy young man.

The spirit of contradiction again played a part in his love affairs. A man of sensibility, he could be enchanted by a mere nothing—the pressure of a hand, hair furtively brushed by the lips, a lingering look, and so on. I would even say that, for a temperament like Beyle's, these slender rewards are preferable to more complete achievements. They sustain it better, leaving the imagination free play. This kind of sentimentality can procure great happiness, but also a twinge of shame that one should be content with so little, especially when debauchery is in fashion. Nothing appears more enviable to a sensitive heart than a reputation for being a Don Juan. I draw all this in broad outlines, but the process is familiar. It must be remembered, however, that with Beyle we are dealing with a man of genius, that is to say a man very eager for sensations and full of daring.

A superior young man of eighteen or twenty, in addition to his own superiorities, longs to beat his companions at their own game, and mere boasting about it is not enough; he must have performed the deeds of prowess on which he prides himself. The style of the young men of the Revolution and the Empire was the "hussar" style. A lad with his heart in the right place must excel at it, just as he was required to be a good horseman and duelist. "If I haven't *also* the qualities of a young man of no talents, I shall be nothing but a pedant," one thinks to oneself—an intolerable thought. This is how one becomes a dandy. Beyle was a dandy in 1801 amid the tatterdemalions of the army in Italy, and in 1813 amid the wreckage of the retreat from Moscow. It was also out of dandyism that he became a grocer in Marseilles in 1805. But I must stop, for psychologizing leads all too quickly to the obvious.

The contradiction between Don Juan and a sensitive heart, deeply rooted in Beyle, accompanied him down to that inevitable reconciliation with oneself which takes place sometime between the ages of thirty and fifty, and which brings a feeling of happiness incomprehensible to the young. Once one has passed this stage, the spirit of contradiction becomes a mere game that one continues to play out of habit, but it has lost its hard edges. With Beyle, the sensitive lover and the hussar alternated for many years. The man we see keeping company with Rosa under a carriage entrance was the same who wrote, "In 1821, love gave me a very comic virtue—chastity." In this line from the *Souvenirs d'égotisme*, everything discloses the spirit of contradiction. Beyle wrote it when he was forty-nine; he was thirty-eight at the time of this comic access of virtue. To be chaste at thirty-eight when nothing compels you to be except an unhappy love affair, and to joke about it eleven years later—here is fine food for thought.

I think that at forty-five Beyle found much amusement in giving a hussar's advice to the young Romantics, the champions of courtly love, and in assuming the airs of a rake. For every Mérimée who listened to him with pleasure and profit, how many horrified faces were there? Finally, I see him as he was at twenty, defending, out of a spirit of contradiction with himself, principles which didn't correspond with his feelings. "Have her; it is first and foremost what you owe her" is a pretty line for a man who had a liking for simple situations and complex emotions.

I have forgotten one essential characteristic. With women, Stendhal displayed the heroism of Julien Sorel, who promised to shoot himself if he didn't take Mme. de Rênal's hand within fifteen minutes. Part of him was a swashbuckler, but part was also Turenne—*"Tremble carcasse! . . ."* The joy and sorrow of ardent souls is their eternal desire to surpass themselves and their failure ever to perceive some difficulty without regarding it as their duty to overcome it on the spot. I imagine that nothing was as opposed to the temperament of a man like Beyle—sensitive to a degree, courting failure through an excess of desire, frozen by a vulgar remark, and so on—as Don Juanism; for that reason it was a conquest all the more to be desired.

I never knew any man who accepted crit-icisms of his work more generously; his friends always used to talk to him with-out any attempt at tact. Several times he sent me manuscripts which he had al-ready submitted to Victor Jacquemont and which had come back with such marginal comments as: "Horrible! Doorkeeper's style!" and so on. When he brought out his book De l'Amour, *we all vied with each other in mak-ing fun of it (most unfairly, when you come down to it); such criticisms never affected his relations with his friends.*

I SEE NOTHING very surprising in this. Stendhal had two quali-ties it would be hard to deny him: complete sincerity and awareness of his genius. If these two qualities don't altogether preclude moments of injured vanity, they make them very transitory. Besides, things that would drive an ordinary man to despair merely serve to stimulate a man of genius. And people sense this, more or less unconsciously. They can never be tact-ful enough toward the untalented wretches who present their stammering little works to the public; they encourage them, write delicate and indulgent reviews about them, hypocriti-cally enthuse over commonplaces and so on. In return, with true artists they sense a strength so superior to their assaults and a vocation so impossible to discourage that they lose all proportion and fling themselves wholeheartedly into the at-tack. It needs an artillery barrage, not to demolish but barely to breach the fifty feet of masonry enclosing the citadel of

Verdun, whereas a match is enough to consume a sheet of paper.

"His friends," says Mérimée. But he mentions only two of them, Jacquemont and himself, namely two remarkable men, one of them "in the trade." It was an admirable thing on Stendhal's part that he recognized Mérimée, so much younger than himself, as his equal, or at least as one of his peers. It is a fact that no writer of Beyle's own generation had enough genius or even talent to follow the complex and sinuous paths of his works. Mérimée, however, possessed all the requisite artistic instinct, and Jacquemont the requisite affinities. This enabled them to grasp the most personal touches, the slightest shades of thought or style. As for the brutal comments in the margin, Mérimée reveals neither the spirit that dictated them nor the feelings with which they were read. Their half-insulting, half-joking nature gives the exact flavor of the friendship which bound the three men together. Deep friendship between men, based on esteem, taste, inclination and so on, always expresses itself in an assumed brusqueness. It is a form of understatement or, if you prefer it, modesty. Such terms as "horrible" or "doorkeeper's style" bespeak a tribal vocabulary, a special language coined by accomplices. They are the exaggerated expression of the subtlest sensibilities. The asperities, errors or platitudes they take to task were invisible to ordinary eyes. That is why Beyle took it all so generously. Every great artist has a rowdy, schoolboy, spontaneous, warmhearted, unaffected side to his character, to which one can say anything one likes, which never takes offense at anything, even the grossest insults—it all depends on the tone. That of Mérimée and Jacquemont suited Stendhal perfectly, however violent and sarcastic it might be, just as the good Bouilhet's tone as he plucked Madame Bovary word by word suited Flaubert. To go into even greater detail, Stendhal and Flaubert never let themselves be deceived over the goods they were offered:

they never confused the vigorous insults of friendship (whose only object is improvement) with the polite perfidies whose only aim is to discourage or destroy.

There is something healthy and comforting about violence in friendship. It is the equivalent, on the intellectual plane, of the fist fights that sometimes break out between youths. After having had a good stand-up fight, the opponents go off for a brotherly drink in a café; their friendship has emerged strengthened from the battle and sustained by a new respect for each other's muscles and courage. What a wonderful feeling friendship is! One accepts anything from a chosen friend without doubting his motives for a moment, because one has found in him a similarity of thought and feeling, because one has recognized him as belonging to the same breed as oneself, a brother in heart and mind. Friendship is a virile emotion; the more harsh and pitiless it appears, the more tender, concerned and affectionate it is underneath. It is like the soul of a young mother in the body of a rhinoceros.

It remains to be seen how Stendhal annotated the works of Mérimée. I suspect, without being able to confirm it, that the expression "doorkeeper's style" was his own, employed precisely with regard to Mérimée.* Everyone surely knows the famous "Mérimée plays only eight notes of his piano"; but the correspondence, too, must be perused. Finally, to get the exact value of all this, I recommend turning to the *Souvenirs d'égotisme;* I defy anyone to read the following without being moved:

---

* "I would be too severe on your style, which I find rather *doorkeeper-ish.* 'I had trouble doing . . .' for 'I found it hard to do. . . .' I often feel in you a Maisonette manner—i.e., a pretty phrase instead of a point . . . you are afraid of being long-winded. This smacks of the bedroom comedy taste of 1829. . . . Often you don't seem *delicately tender enough,* and a novel has to have that quality to move me." (Letter from Beyle to Mérimée, December 26, 1828.)

There was something impertinent and extremely unattractive about this young man. His small and expressionless eyes always had the same look in them and that look was malicious. Such was my first sight of one who is now my best friend. I am not too sure of his heart, but I am sure of his talents; he is M. le Comte Gazul, who is today so well known, and from whom I received a letter last week that made me happy for two whole days.

This was written in 1832, when Beyle was forty-nine and the Comte Gazul [Mérimée] twenty-eight or twenty-nine. A letter capable of making someone happy for two days needs no comment. Only a love letter is superior to it in its effects.

The general "and when you come down to it, most unfair" mockery of *De l'Amour* seems to me above all a convention. In certain circles it is understood that compliments are never paid but that banter is the only and abiding rule. Compliments are held to be ridiculous or are regarded as weakness. This implies enormous conceit for a start, a conviction that here is a little clan of highly superior persons, and that the mere fact of belonging to this clan constitutes such an honor and betokens such great merit that it is beyond the most extravagant praise.

He wrote much and worked over his books at great length, but instead of correcting their manner of writing, he reconstructed the plot. If he abolished the faults of a first draft, it was only to make others, for to the best of my knowledge he never attempted to correct his style; however much his manuscripts were scratched and scored, one may say that they were always written quite spontaneously.

His letters are charming, the very echo of his conversation.

Sᴘᴏɴᴛᴀɴᴇᴏᴜꜱ writing has a bad reputation. The professors of literature, the gentlemen of the Sorbonne, the commentators and critics have discredited it for the past hundred and fifty years. They demand picturesque manuscripts, full of erasures and second thoughts, variants, first, second, third and fourth "versions"; they want art to smell of the midnight oil. If it doesn't bear the stigmata of hard work, it is suspect.

The spectacle of an artist who has "worked" comforts and consoles the pedants. I imagine they tell themselves something like this: "My God, what trouble he's gone to! And how modest he is! He didn't trust his talent, that famous talent everyone talks about and which doesn't in fact exist, since I can never get any idea of it myself. Talent is simply a lot of hard work. Take me, for instance—if I weren't so lazy, if I set myself down to *work*, well, I could write *Hamlet*. A question of time. Ah, what beautiful things I would produce if I had the time. Time and a capacity for work, that's all it amounts to."

When you come down to it, only two methods exist in art: the shifting of masses and the polishing of details. Leonardo spent three years fiddling over the "Mona Lisa." During that time Michelangelo painted two hundred pictures. I don't maintain that the "Mona Lisa" is inferior to "The Last Judgment" in the Sistine Chapel, but, taking their geniuses to be equal, I can't help finding the world of Michelangelo vaster, richer, more fertile and more *diverting* than that of Leonardo. Shall I confess it? I always visualize Madame Bovary as looking exactly like the Gioconda. To my eyes, the celebrated Gioconda smile, her pretty hands, the little landscape behind her have something Norman about them. M. Homais is not far off. Flaubert, who took three years to paint Emma Bovary with tiny brush strokes, inch by inch, belongs to the same family as Leonardo.

Everyone knows Balzac's story "Le Chef-d'œuvre inconnu," in which the old painter Frenhofer works so long over a picture that it ends by being nothing but a hodgepodge of colors and incomprehensible lines, from which only a delicious woman's foot—a living foot—emerges. All artists like Leonardo have a tendency toward the unknown masterpiece. The pitfalls of art are legion; one can't even trust oneself to plain work. It leads to failures as resounding as laziness does. Genius though he was, poor Frenhofer was the dupe of hard work. Great artists, like great politicians, have to give way to all kinds of trickery, calculation and cowardice if they wish to create an enduring work. When I read "Le Chef-d'œuvre inconnu" I constantly deplored the honest toiling of Frenhofer; I raged against his "Vincism." Instead of ruining his picture through an excess of zeal, why didn't the man redo it ten or twenty times on as many different canvases? A work of art is not indefinitely perfectible. A moment comes when the cord snaps, when the upward curve starts to redescend. One must know when to stop; one must know the limits of one's creative power. Rivarol refers to writers who make the springs of the language creak. Overzealous artists only contrive to make the springs of art creak. The neurosis of hard work is as baneful as facility.

Stendhal was the anti-Leonardo, the anti-Flaubert, the anti-Frenhofer. He repainted the same picture ten times, but on different canvases. Nothing prevented him from selecting the best one for posterity. This craftiness is necessary if one wishes to live on. The best canvas is usually the tenth, but not always. At any rate, it is still, as Mérimée says, a spontaneous work in which everything is started again from the very beginning, by a fresh hand. Flaubert polished the details ad infinitum and made a literature for myopics. His books resemble overfinished paintings, which glitter too brightly in places but which, by dint of imperceptible modifications, have become dull as a whole. Great art consists in preserving, amid the corrections, that spontaneity which is, properly speaking, style—that is to say, the author's way of breathing, the beat of his pulse, the inimitable form of his thought when it is born. Stendhal superbly shows the way to achieve this. When Venus rises out of the water, she gives a divine smile, far more bewitching than that of the Gioconda. Flaubert rubs her face so hard that he wipes off the smile. Stendhal merely caresses her cheek; a few drops of salt water remain, of course, but the smile is intact, perhaps even emphasized.

One can understand how the pedants detest spontaneous writers. Spontaneity is discouraging. It furnishes dazzling proof that talent does exist, that if need be it could suffice unto itself, without hard work. They revenge themselves by making idiotic pronouncements which impress the public—for example, that Balzac wrote badly, or that Victor Hugo was stupid. It is only within the past sixty years that they do Stendhal the honor of admiring his manner.

Great writers write as they talk, or talk as they write, I don't know which exactly. The fact is, they talk well. The letter, like the private diary, is halfway between writing and talking, a little more casual than the first, a little more contrived than the second; but the music is the same. The same stylishness, the same short cuts, the same tricks, the same pleasant or profound flashes of insight. Beyle's letters are delightful; they echo his conversation. I will take the liberty of adding this to Mérimée: they echo his books. He never changes his tone whether he is addressing posterity or the Baron de Mareste. *La Chartreuse de Parme*, *Le Rouge et le Noir* and *Lucien Leuwen* are vast letters sent into the future and passionately read and reread by their millions of addressees. How Madame Bovary, on the other hand, suffers by comparison with Flaubert's letters! The brilliance, life, intelligence and love to be found in the letters leave one sighing for the things Flaubert might have done had he been a spontaneous writer. But Flaubert believed that one must yell for posterity to listen to one. His yelling still deafens sensitive ears.

10

He was very gay in society, sometimes extravagant and overneglectful of the proprieties and people's susceptibilities. He was often in bad taste, but always witty and original. Although he had no consideration for anyone, he was easily hurt by remarks dropped with no thought of malice. "I am a playful puppy," he used to tell me, "and I get bitten." He forgot that he himself sometimes bit, pretty hard; the fact is, he hardly appreciated that anyone could hold opinions different from his own on things and men. For example, to him a priest and a royalist were always hypocrites.

THIS IS a good analysis of the man of genius in society. He bites because it is in his nature to bite, like the lion. His mistake comes from believing that he is only attacking dead meat. But stupidity is not dead meat; it is living flesh, whose owner gives a piercing shriek and revenges himself by biting back. The bites given by genius are healthy. Those of stupidity are venomous. The weapons are ill-matched.

People of high intelligence have a blind modesty; they naïvely think that intelligence is the common lot; they set their nets too high and the small fry slip under them. So it is rare for them not to return with an empty bag from their forays into society. I fear that Mérimée wasn't always tall enough to be caught in Beyle's nets, even if he escaped them only by a hairbreadth. "Bad taste," coming from him, shocks me. I see what sort of bad taste he meant; I translate it as exuberance, a wealth of feelings and ideas, a flood of remarks that were odd and true but of a paradoxical appeal. Add that Beyle, always sure of being witty and profound, never hesitated to talk too long and even to cut other people short. Perhaps he naïvely roared with laughter at his own jokes? Quite devoid of susceptibility himself, he couldn't attribute it to anyone else. That is never forgiven. When one says, "You are a fool!" more or less clearly to a real fool, the latter hardly appreciates that one is addressing him as an equal, that one is allowing him more wit than he has and, in short, paying him a tribute. On the contrary, he thinks, "This man is striking me where I am vulnerable; he is trying to humiliate me; vengeance be mine!" The riposte, then, is really unkind.

When Mérimée writes "bad taste" I hear the "gentleman" speaking, which annoys me. Nothing can be more charming than a gentleman, but sometimes being the gentleman is out of place, particularly when destiny sets a man like Beyle in your path. Then you must be humble; you must say to yourself, "This man is wonderful in every respect, and if he strikes me as being in bad taste, it is because I don't understand; something escapes me." For want of which, however witty you may be, you assume the comically superior air of parents condemning the inconsistencies of their children. In spite of a touch of parody and great affection, this air, adopted by Mérimée toward Stendhal, strikes me as showing a want of taste, or of soul, which comes to the same thing.*

---

* Here are two passages from Stendhal that Mérimée didn't know:

I am not saying that . . . Judge de Barral . . . was a genius, but in my eyes he was so far the opposite of my father and had such a horror of pedantry and of wounding his son's self-esteem that, when they left the house to go for a walk in the wastelands of the Drac, if the father said: *"Bonjour,"* the son replied: *"Toujours,"* the father: *"Oie,"* the son: *"Lamproie,"* and the whole walk was spent making up rhymes and trying to top each other.

Every mark of character or originality, every rather forceful idea, every genuine feeling is looked on as bad form in Parisian society, which achieves the miracle of being at once insipid and enchanting. "Good form," that colorless idol as smooth and academic as one of Voltaire's tragedies, arouses fanatical passions. This hasn't changed since Stendhal's day. Certainly men of wit are appreciated, but what is demanded is an inferior wit without poetry, made up of catty remarks, epigrams and racy and superficial judgments.

Don't think that I disapprove of "good form"; on the contrary, I like it and enjoy it. I know, I feel, its hermetic language, its tribal jargon; I obey its rules. I sincerely think that "good form" is a work of art, an exquisite social edifice in the heart of which many people live very happily. Finally, of all the conventions, "good form" is the one which contrives the most pleasures and liberties. With urbane people who, whether due to indifference or to frivolity, are almost unfailingly dis-

---

This father taught his son the *Satires* of Voltaire (the only perfect thing that great reformer wrote, in my view).

This was my first glimpse of true "good form" and it won me then and there.

—Vie de Henry Brulard

M. Widmann, who was a bit of a prince of the Empire, I think, although related by marriage to the Rezzonico family . . . had as much of the polished manners of high society as his Italian nature permitted.

These polished manners, which would have disconcerted me ten years earlier, put me at ease; and with him I displayed the most noble, polite and zealous good form.

In this respect, I can be pleased with myself and leave the talking to my friends, who don't understand my manner.

Success justified it. When we parted, he waited for a coach to pass and walked fifty yards to take his leave and shake my hand.

—Journal, 1811.

In 1811, Mérimée was eight. The episode with M. de Barral took place in about 1795.

creet, one is less exposed to being hurt than elsewhere. But there are times when one gets bored, times when one sighs for some impropriety to refresh one. Stendhal had a vivid personality and improprieties cost him nothing. He took into the salons the powerful ideas and daring expressions one finds in his books; perhaps he *tried out* in society the developments of ideas which he preserved to be written down afterward, yielding to the illusion that the person he was talking to was a reader who read with his ears. To use his own phrase, it must have had the effect of a pistol fired in the middle of a concert, or of veritable artillery if he was in high spirits. A man of genius, once launched on a series of comic or profound remarks, shoots down the conversation; he is never forgiven for such murder. The man who joyfully greets poetry in a book will not tolerate it in society, where it jars like an unbearable discord. To be in a salon where twenty people are making animated conversation, laughing and throwing up dust clouds of words which scatter into thin air, and then suddenly to hear the music of true thoughts expressed in happy or evocative phrases—that is calculated to put you in a rage. Styles must never be mixed! Bad form consists of mixing styles—for example, of introducing a note of seriousness where only banter is allowed, and vice versa.

I think, finally, that Stendhal played the role of Baudelaire's albatross quite effectively. His giant wings prevented him from walking, and when he wanted to fly he collided with the chandelier. In other words, he talked too much, he was too brilliant, too fierce, like a young dog or a young lion, relentless in his monologues on the Jesuits, or the two parliamentary Chambers, or Louis Philippe, or the stupidity of the liberals. He went to the heart of a subject when he should have only skimmed it; he spoke truths when he was required only to speak paradoxes.

I can imagine that Mérimée, who had *pinched* "good form"

to a marvelous degree and played at it like a virtuoso, allowing himself all the permitted insolence, omitting none of the sanctioned grossness and having carefully trimmed his originality to fit the measurements of society, trembled every time he had to take Beyle with him. After fifteen minutes Beyle's rich nature burst all the seams of conversation. Not that he refused to play the game, but the inanity of the game must have been apparent to him and imbued him with a sort of metaphysical panic; and this gave rise to startling aphorisms and uncompromising and ready opinions based on a wide experience, which his companions hardly possessed.

"Very gay in society, sometimes extravagant. . . ." A man who writes for several hours a day easily succumbs to the naïve belief that going into society is an outing. Apart from his writing, nothing seems to him to be of any importance. His six or eight pages done, he allows himself time off. The essential thing is behind him; the rest is laughter and entertainment. Why not display extravagance in a salon, since one is there to enjoy oneself? Not to mention the energy and gaiety with which one is filled after the completion of eight pages. Artists are by definition solitary people, for one cannot create in company. Five hours of solitude engender a tremendous appetite for society; they give the desire to see one's own kind the time to reawaken. Besides, a romantic nature always fosters illusions as to the exciting people it will assuredly meet. Will it be a pretty, not too foolish woman, a man with three startling ideas, a careerist, a flirt or a rather compliant poetess? And so on. It is very agreeable, after having trailed about in a dressing gown up to 6 P.M. and composed half a chapter of a novel, to prink oneself and put on one's best bib and tucker, with the prospect of a brilliant dinner party and the chance to talk one's head off afterward. There is something lustrous about the women one meets in society, halfway between a human creature and an object of art, which is very delightful. One is lighthearted, lightheaded and sure one will seduce someone. Stendhal, who was always so ready to teach that one has to bore and be bored, must have antagonized masses of people in his life with his jokes, his running fire of epigrams, stories and wisecracks. Usually one leaves such parties with a taste of ashes in one's mouth if one has but a smattering of wit, for nothing is more empty than the conversation, nor more fruitless than these gatherings; but the disappointment melts away in twenty-four hours. The next week one is as delighted as ever to go and parade in a cinnamon-brown coat and silk stockings.

That Stendhal couldn't understand that people might hold opinions different from his own on things and men is quite natural. Great men habitually have this modesty. They forget the arguments, judgments and endless deductions they have been through to reach the simple and correct notions which form the body of their philosophy. When a man is accustomed to see things in their true light and not to lie to himself, he is always astonished by the ardor people put into refuting what is obvious.

Teasing friendships are the surest. But teasing, however affectionate, leads to curtness. When Mérimée gives as an example of Beyle's intolerance his view that all priests and royalists were hypocrites, he is teasing him posthumously and he is curt. Today royalists and priests mean nothing any more. The Church and the monarchy are so forgotten that there is no more advantage to be had from adhering to them. But under the Restoration, royalism and piety led to everything. I don't say that all royalists and priests were hypocrites, but at any rate there must have been many hypocrites among them. And what did Stendhal mean by this word? A hypocrite is a man who advertises sentiments he doesn't feel, with the object of self-promotion. The way hypocrites talk is either funny or repellent, depending on whether one is feeling gay or bitter. They endlessly repeat the doctrines of the party on which they are counting for their advancement. It is easy to imagine the way the average royalist or priest talked in 1835; it must have been nauseating.

Were he still alive, Stendhal would find his hypocrites elsewhere. The paths to success alter with each period or change of fashion. To my mind, one of the most successful hypocrites today is the humanitarian liberal who flourishes in certain pink newspapers or writes depressing novels about the emancipation of the lower orders. When he is in the Chamber he votes, with a breaking heart, with the Right.

His opinions on the arts and literature were held to be daring heresies when he produced them. When he placed Mozart, Cimarosa and Rossini above the opera makers of our youth, he raised a hurricane of protest; it was then that he was accused of not having French feelings.

STENDHAL, who wrote in 1830 for the men of 1890, had the eyes and ears of these later men. To judge works (or events) sixty years ahead of the times presupposes a breadth of mind, a taste, a contempt for illusions and an indifference to fashions and "trends" that are quite exceptional. These qualities lay a man open to being pre-eminently misunderstood. They are thankless qualities. One should have a soul of iron and carefully conceal them. A man who is right twenty years in advance of everyone else and who is a pitiless judge, like posterity, is regarded as either spiteful or an idiot, as envious or a lunatic. But when one knows the truth one brings disgrace on oneself if one doesn't speak it, if one joins the chorus of liars. That is the very mark of hypocrisy. How can any man do that when he loathes hypocrites? Courage is a delectable sin; temerity is the pastime of ardent spirits. Isn't it quite a simple matter to prefer Mozart to Boieldieu or Grétry, and to say so? Good taste and love of the truth generate a passion for justice. This complicates life considerably.

Like great men in every age, Stendhal was not a man of his time. He did not fit into the "literary panorama of the years

1800-1840." The almanac makers left him out of their catalogues. Impossible to classify a writer who touched on everything and said so many unexpected things without wordy preparation. Art criticism, travel diaries, thoughts on music, biographies of musicians and poets, theories about love, novels —it is too much for one man. Not to mention Stendhal's romantic Bonapartism or, if you prefer it, his Carbonarism. Briefly, he was not in the fashion. He never was, in his lifetime. To be in the fashion he would have had to be a royalist and a clerical, just as today one has to be a progressive and an atheist—at the very least, a Christian progressive. I don't know if Beyle's republican and atheist sympathies were deep-rooted and, so to speak, "fundamental." It was in any case tempting for a man afflicted with the spirit of contradiction to profess them in a monarchistic and bigoted society. Dangerous too, no doubt, but the spirit of contradiction lives as naturally in danger as a fish in water.

When I say that Stendhal was not of his time, I mean that he didn't regard himself as a Frenchman of 1830 but as a member of that family of great men which is scattered throughout the centuries. He used the optic nerve of posterity as much to observe himself as others. His yardstick was not Victor Cousin, Charles Nodier, Joseph de Maistre (to mention only familiar names and, by and large, respectable writers) but Molière or Shakespeare, or Montesquieu, or Horace. These were the men with whom he fell into line. In other words, he created for himself a certain idea of art which was not the contingent one of his own time but the highest one of all time, since only the greatest men survive and they, in a certain sense, are all alike.

The France of 1840 was solemn, pedantic and stupid, just like France today. A host of fools devoid of style were laying down the law; Stendhal's tone was an anomaly, he was unique. Yet it is in that selfsame tone that the France of 1840 speaks to us, her children. That is how writers who are not in the fashion take their revenge. In spite of everything, these impostors become the spokesmen of the period which misunderstood them. They dress it up in fine clothes for the eyes of posterity. They endow it with the spirit of truly glorious epochs. (Or they paint it in the grand manner, like Balzac.) Posterity is not democratic; it retains only the least representative!

He was nonetheless very French in his opinions on painting, although he claimed to judge it as an Italian. He appreciated the masters with French ideas, that is to say from the literary point of view. He approached the pictures of the Italian schools as if they were dramas. That is still the way people judge pictures in France, where they have neither a feeling for form nor a natural taste for color. It needs a special sensitivity and long practice to love and understand form and color. Beyle attributed dramatic passions to a Virgin by Raphael. I have always suspected that he loved the great artists of the Lombard and Florentine schools because their works reminded him of many things which probably never occurred to those masters. It is the peculiarity of the French that they judge everything by the mind. It is only fair to add that there is no language with which to express the subtleties of form or the variety of the effects of color. For want of ability to express what one feels, one describes other sensations which everybody can understand.*

*D*IDEROT, according to a perceptive remark of Sainte-Beuve's, introduced the French public "to color through ideas." In this respect Stendhal was his pupil. But to make every picture tell a story is a notion very far removed from painting. Only with

---

* These lines of Mérimée's are repeated almost word for word by Sainte-Beuve in his article on Diderot (Monday, January 20, 1851) [in his *Premiers Lundis*—Tr.].

64

the bad painters does the anecdote take precedence over expression, poetry and style. Diderot is highly and unintentionally comic when he "narrates" Greuze. To introduce color through ideas is to choose the worst door. Besides, it doesn't lead anywhere. Degas wanted to enter through this door into poetry. Apparently he complained one day to Mallarmé that he couldn't bring off a poem. "Yet I'm full of ideas," he said. "One doesn't make poems with ideas," replied Mallarmé sagely, "but with words."

Mérimée's analysis is very apposite. It is true that no language can express the subtleties of form and the variety of the effects of color. Every art has its own literally untranslatable language. Nothing is more absurd than the poetico-technical jargon employed by the art critics, or by bad painters when they try to explain themselves. It is true, too, that it is the peculiarity of the French to judge everything by the mind. This intellectualism or, rather, this inclination for philosophy, does painters, musicians and poets great harm. They put intentions, *meanings*, into their works, and this makes them either dry or stupid.

Stendhal, for all his sensibility, only understood painting as a man of letters of the eighteenth century. He had better taste than Diderot and Musset. Let but Baudelaire appear, however, and *L'Histoire de la peinture en Italie* seems no more than the clever work of a fine intellect, unfortunately born forty years too soon and still a victim of academic prejudices.

Let us be fair. Diderot and Stendhal, with their sentimental criticism which so frequently rises to the level of a confession or a novel, glimpsed something that no one before them had suspected: that one can construct a work of art on another work of art, and that nature is not the one and only model for artists. Oscar Wilde brilliantly developed and applied this much later.

I think that, with Stendhal, love of Italian painting sprang from a love of Italy. After all, nowhere does that country express herself better than in her painting. Stendhal saw in it the wonderful chronicle, made by the greatest artists, of the chosen land of his heart. He cherished the model before the manner—namely, that world of pretty women, thin young men in doublets and old men with flinty eyes, those rows of palaces and colonnades, those cities neither wholly real nor wholly imaginary, which fill the vast diorama of Italian painting from Giotto to Tiepolo. Since the manner is not inferior to the matter, one can't accuse him of being mistaken in his admiration for it. Finally, it was not his concern to enjoy painting for good reasons. In this way I myself, a lesser figure but a man of letters for all that, fall into a similar error with music. I like it to tell a story. I have to have eloquence, sweetness, mysteries, confessions, cries of triumph, gaiety, tenderness, melancholy. I can barely understand Debussy and his little impressionistic scenes. Ravel, Stravinsky, Prokofieff and Darius Milhaud appeal to me when I recognize emotions and a story in their music. But this is the very failing denounced by Mérimée; for want of ability to express what I feel, I am describing other sensations.

He cared more for Canova's sculpture than for any other, even Greek statuary; perhaps this was because Canova worked for literary people. He was far more concerned with the thoughts he might conjure up in a cultivated mind than with the impression he might create on an eye which loved and understood form.

*T*o work for literary people is a terrible accusation. This means that one is more of a philosopher than an artist, that one puts allusions, symbols, allegories, schemes and knowing winks into one's work. In short, it means one is a pedant. The artist who works for literary people compensates for an inadequate or barren imagination by references, parodies and disguised quotations. Nor are his products lacking in charm: they have the piquant appeal of careless and elegant erudition which flatters those to whom it is addressed and refrains from naming its sources. One can see a thousand examples of it today, when almost everyone works for literary people. Picasso paints for them alone. Léautaud wrote somewhere, "I am only a writer for literary people," but in a different sense, just as a mathematician might say, "You have to be a mathematician to read me."

With Canova, we are in a lower region of art, ruled over by deftness, flashiness and sleight of hand, but aimed at distinguished minds. Canova can easily take one in. One can sincerely admire his sculpture with the feeling that one is admiring work of quality. I am sure there are people so simple as to be upset by the fact that Beyle let himself be taken in by it. They want great men to be all of one piece, sublime throughout. Stendhal was a superb artist, a writer of genius. Isn't that enough? No. He must needs also be infallible in his judgments on the arts. It wasn't his business to have good taste; that was of no importance. Hugo understood nothing about music, but that didn't prevent him from being as great a poet as Dante. Stendhal's admiration for Canova didn't lead him to put either pretty frills or gimcrack antiques into *La Chartreuse de Parme*. Whether a great artist has good or bad taste is quite irrelevant. Bad taste is as nutritious as good, and all nourishment is beneficial to a powerful organism which assimilates and immediately transforms what it absorbs.

There is something touching about a great man's weaknesses. It is thanks to them that we less fortunate mortals can approach him. Goethe's thirst for honors, as a government minister in an operetta world, his gaudy decorations and fine clothes, bring me considerably closer to him. This frippery to which he attached such importance increases the pleasure I get from reading *Faust*, *Goetz* or *Egmont*. I think of the councilor to the Grand Duke, of his ribbons, frills and furbelows, and I feel much less discouraged by his immaculate works. An ignoble sentiment, certainly, but I am a man and, like Pascal, I am fond of seeing the men behind the books. Not to mention that a little weakness amid so much strength is a charming mixture.

To carry my thought through to the end, I would be most annoyed if Stendhal hadn't been frequently mistaken in his enthusiasms. I take great pleasure in granting him Canova. I even encourage him in this reprehensible tendency. Love of Canova was a memory of his youth. Canova was part and parcel of the Empire style; he formed part of the Napoleonic pomp and exaltation. One has a right to cherish a fond memory for Canova when one has been through the retreat from Moscow. The marble bust of Pauline Bonaparte is inseparable from Austerlitz and Wagram; these are the two extreme aspects of an exceptional adventure—its beguiling face and its tragic one. Artists live 'way outside their time, but their souls are shaped no differently from those of other men; there is nothing to be found in their hearts that is not in the hearts of all their generation. Only the lighting and splendor are different. Canova, under Stendhalian lighting, acquires a strange grandeur and beauty. Stendhal's memory gives his insipid statues exquisite forms; it metamorphoses them; it makes them naturalized Stendhalians.

Bad taste and unwarranted enthusiasms are as precious for artists as what psychoanalysts call complexes, which it is so dangerous (or useless) to root out.

*The police of the Empire lurked every-
where, or so it is claimed, and Fouché
knew what everyone was saying. Beyle
was convinced that this gigantic spy system had preserved all its occult power
. . . All his friends had their pseudo-
nyms, and he never addressed them by any other name. No one
ever knew exactly what people he saw, what books he had
written, what journeys he had made.*

DEATH is a projector; it leaves no secret in the dark. So
mysterious for the living who knew him, Stendhal in death is
one of the most transparent men in French history. It is hard to
conceive that a man whose thoughts, actions and loves are so
familiar to us could have seemed baffling to those around him.
In the same way, biographers in the year 2000, who will have
read all the private papers of Montherlant, for example, will be
almost unable to understand how this writer could appear
such an enigma to his contemporaries.

To live with a secret is intoxicating. A secret is a kind of
treasure, since everyone is lying in wait to steal it. Added to
which, gossip spreads in a flash. The man who keeps his secrets
feels a keen and constant pleasure by this very act; he ceaselessly offers himself proof of his strength of character, of his
contempt for vanity. The joys of discretion are sometimes
overwhelming. Those who have known them desire no other.
It is, of course, flattering—to take the most current example
—to be *known* as a pretty woman's lover, but one feels a hap-

piness a thousand times more intense if one keeps one's good fortune strictly unsuspected. Secrecy multiplies the delights of love. And this isn't true only for love. A secret superiority is sometimes more satisfying than a recognized superiority. There are certain proud characters who dispense with the sanction of society, do everything to encourage it in its error, even gladly welcome its unfavorable judgment. A single gesture on their part might undeceive the world and bring them fame, but they do not make it. To live unrecognized by one's century is a proof of spirit and rare pride. One is as amazed by the low opinions Saint-Simon's contemporaries had of that prodigious writer, the equal of Balzac and Proust, as one is by the unswerving secrecy he kept over his memoirs until his death. During that time, they hailed as a great man a second-rate moralist like La Rochefoucauld, who played paper games in the salons.*

There was something of Saint-Simon in Stendhal. Discretion is not enough to explain secrecy; there must also be an inclination to it. Fouché's police existed, no doubt, but his temperament needed only this excuse. Stendhal must have had great fun with his nicknames, his mysteries, precautions and pseudonyms. I think he was fully aware of the picturesqueness of the English and Italian phrases with which he filled his private writings. Moreover, his whole life shows that he was indiscretion itself. Given just a little of that diplomacy and calculation he describes so well, his life would have been much happier and more successful. He played at mysteries more than he actually made them. The true man of mysteries was Talleyrand, and he didn't end up as consul at Civitavecchia and poor into the bargain. He made millions on the stock exchange, he

---

* The opposite of Saint-Simon and Stendhal was named André Gide; he spent his life advertising it and published his *Journal* as he wrote it. Posterity, I fear, will cruelly punish this complacent chitchat.

ruled Europe, and his brains were thrown into the gutter.

When he spoke of occult power and a gigantic spy system, Stendhal was making poetry. He had the same admiration for Fouché as he had for Canova: Fouché again meant Napoleon, his youth and the best years of his life. But his mistrust was not as absurd as Mérimée suggests. Napoleon had gone, but Fouché lived on. With the Restoration, the police of the Empire and all that went to make it became a thing of the past. In describing how the first persons he saw with Louis XVIII were "vice leaning on crime"—Talleyrand and Fouché—Chateaubriand showed that in 1815 "France was carrying on," a certain kind of France, authoritarian and not the best of Frances. From the heritage of Napoleon the Bourbons took over only the worst. The glory and the grandeur were not passed on. Vice and crime, on the other hand, can be served up indefinitely. What a wonderful caricaturist Chateaubriand was, and how true! Those two imperial ruins, those two old scoundrels bracing each other up in a salon of the Tuileries, those two regicides with the King—to call them Vice and Crime was a piece of comic genius.

A man like Fouché "makes" a police force, which outlives him. He has created spies, and they have created others in their turn. His spirit was not exorcised until around 1865, when Badinguet* became liberal. Working for the Revolution and the Empire, Fouché preserved some grandeur in the midst of his crimes. In the service of the Bourbons the grandeur vanished. There was no longer any *cause*. The police ceased to be merely one means among many others for upholding the triumph of the country and the new ideas; they became an instrument of power. Up to 1814, the police force in one sense was the ally of the people; after that, it once again became their enemy.

---

* The nickname given by the republicans to Napoleon III.—Tr.

Thanks to various biographers, and in particular to M. Martineau, Stendhal has no more secrets today. The work carried out over a period of forty or fifty years by M. Martineau has been much admired. He has studied Stendhal through a magnifying glass, he has slaved to reconstruct the most insignificant events of his life. This is certainly praiseworthy. But for my part I have never been able to admire M. Martineau for this work. To me it seems strangely futile, and I suspect that Stendhal would have made much fun of this passion. The older I grow, the less use I find for meticulously detailed history. The legend is quite sufficient and sometimes to be preferred. Another thing always astounds me when I read a book by M. Martineau: how is it that fifty years of militant Stendhalism never managed to give this author a little style? However passionate my interest in Stendhal, I confess that I cannot read any of M. Martineau's revelations about him without profound boredom. All these minute details, all this precision so flatly and heavily imparted, depress me to death. For me, the man of mystery is not Stendhal but M. Martineau. Judging by his way of writing and his reflections (and there is no appeal against such judgments)—judging, that is to say, from his soul and his internal melody, I cannot understand his love for Stendhal. They are two strangers.

I imagine that some critic in the twentieth century will discover Beyle's books amid the welter of nineteenth-century literature and that he will pay them the just tribute they never found with his contemporaries. It was in this way that Diderot's reputation spread in the nineteenth century, in this way that Shakespeare, forgotten in the time of Saint-Évremond, was discovered by Garrick. It is sincerely to be hoped that Beyle's letters will one day be published; they would foster knowledge and love of a man whose mind and fine qualities live on only in the memories of a small number of his friends.

THERE IS no merit in being a prophet when one knows the underside of the cards. One can no more deceive an artist on his art than a tailor on cloth or a garage owner on a car. In literature there are always twenty or thirty people in every century who know the underside of the cards, who know with sure knowledge what will live and what will die. There also exist certain little fixed principles. For example, writers without style die young, however sublime or original their ideas. A badly written idea is a false idea. That is harsh, but true. I always feel sad when I envisage the future of five or six of my colleagues who are very famous today and make the world resound with their ideas. These ideas are badly written: they will crumble away in twenty years, like buildings made of plaster, jerry-built and designed to house too many people. Another principle: one must have a love of truth. The specious arguments dictated by the passions, the theories and "trends of thought" into which one lets oneself idly or voluptuously digress, unfailingly lead to one stream, that of oblivion. The ideas of an age live on only as historical curiosities. Few people take the trouble to go and ferret for them in the attics of the Musée Carnavalet. Ordinary writers all stare in the same direction, where there is usually nothing to see. The great writers look elsewhere, to where the eternal, monotonous but at the same time deliciously varied spectacle of universal ideas is being played out.

Stendhal's ideas and style were very alien to the France of 1830. Their dryness, their ring of truth, their simplicity, charm or profundity place them in the ranks of things that endure. Stendhal, whom it cost no more to make prophecies than it did Mérimée, had likewise predicted that people would begin to read him in 1890. A highly intelligent man who never lies to himself and who, besides, writes with extreme precision has every reason to trust in the judgment of posterity. Mérimée saw very clearly that Stendhal, having so many curious or unfamiliar things to say, never wrote in order to say nothing. His sentences drive one to despair, for they are never too long. I don't think I have ever once lit on a superfluous word, one of those words which cost so little to writers launched on some opus. He begins without preamble and stops dead. He needn't blush for any useless metaphor, any unnecessary adjective. Had he not had so many ideas and such a wealth of emotions, this economy of speech would pass for poverty. Stendhal's writing is as natural as a cat or a frog. This style so utterly devoid of pose performs the miracle of not being invisible. It is the thoughts that give it its asperities; it is the truth of what he says that gives it its contours. When Stendhal pins down a truth in his books like a butterfly caught on the wing (and this happens several times on every page), one feels him swelling with a joy that is echoed in his style, and it is this which makes it such an endless delight to read him.

When I order a new suit, I choose the cloth I like least and the cut which strikes me as most unsuited to my body. I feel all the better for this, since I have a natural bad taste and I lay it down as a principle that I like only what is ugly. I proceed in exactly the same way when I correct the books I write. I methodically strike out everything that gives me pleasure: unusual words, daring or striking images, melodious phrases. I leave in only what bores me, and this is obviously the least bad. Sometimes I have moments of weakness which I repent of three months later, when the book is printed. Thus in *Five A.M.*, a work for which I have retained a certain affection, I didn't have the courage to cross out a mannered metaphor in the taste of the day: "Night casts a black veil over my mind, the way one throws a cloth over a bird cage." This couldn't fail: M. Wurmser* found it to be the only good thing in the book.

I have searched in vain through Stendhal's works, I have found nothing of which their author might repent. Not one foolish turn of phrase. Not one stupid remark. Nothing which seems to have given him pleasure. As a result, unmitigated pleasure for the reader. Every word written by Stendhal, austere, disobliging, inflexible as justice, tickles posterity in the right spot. Happy man, he is never *pretty*. Always beautiful.

There is invisible style and invisible style: one is like the Emperor's clothes, and one is like the costumes of Beau Brummel. The Emperor, naked, appeared to everyone by mutual consent to be dressed. Brummel, clad with insane fastidiousness, appeared naked by collective illusion. Sainte-Beuve, his gaze fixed on the fleeting spectacles of his time, admired the

---

* Literary critic of the weekly *Les lettres françaises.*—Tʀ.

Emperor's clothes more than those of Brummel, which are those of Stendhal's ideas.

I imagine that some critic in the twenty-first century will discover the books of Béatrix Beck and Alexandre Vialatte amid the welter of twentieth-century literature, and that he will pay them the just tribute they have not found among their contemporaries. People will object that Béatrix Beck won the Prix Goncourt, but who remembers that? She was famous for eight weeks; the public has read only one book by her, and not her best one. It is sincerely to be hoped that Vialatte's stories will one day be published in book form. They would foster knowledge and love of a mind full of a wholly original poetry and fantasy, a sort of French Hoffmann but possibly richer and sometimes profound, with ludicrous ideas, such as occur only to great minds.

16

I first met Beyle in about 1820; from that time up to his death, in spite of the difference in our ages, our relations were always intimate and constant. Few men have pleased me more; there is no one whose friendship has been more precious to me. Apart from a few predilections and dislikes in literature, we had perhaps not a single idea in common, and there were few subjects on which we ever agreed. We spent our time arguing with each other with the best faith in the world, each suspecting the other of stubbornness and paradox; the best of friends, withal, and always delighted to recommence our disputes.

THIS PARAGRAPH brings a lump to my throat. In its way, I find it as moving as Montaigne's regrets for La Boétie. For this it is necessary to know Mérimée—always cold, always standoffish, encased in modesty like a bowman in his coat of mail. Jules Renard tells a story which I have loved ever since I first read it in his *Journal* twenty years ago: A man (Was it Capus, Tristan Bernard, Lucien Guitry or Renard himself? I no longer remember) meets one of his friends. "How are you?" he says. "Not so well, actually," replies the friend. "My wife has broken her arm, my son has caught syphilis, my daughter's in the family way; as for me, not only have I financial worries, but my health is bothering me: sciatica, headaches, a weak bladder . . ." "My dear fellow," the other interrupts, "when I ask you how you are, it is for you to reply, 'Very well, thanks, and you?' I don't give a damn for your sciatica or your wife's arm."

Mérimée is the man who invariably replies, "Very well, thanks, and you?" He is a gentleman who never bores anyone with his weak bladder and his financial worries. He knows it is the height of stupidity to complacently give one's news to someone who doesn't listen. One has to translate Mérimée constantly to get a true idea of the state of his heart, unless one has a propensity for understatement oneself, unless one has a feeling for an excessively circumspect manner of expression. Mérimée is almost like the language of the eyes. The most beautiful things are never said, and are all the more beautiful for being divined. I have a passion for writers of this kind—writers wholly alien to lyricism, who barely describe anything and confine themselves to saying, as they show you the Pyramid of Cheops for example: "Look over there, there's an interesting building." Such a feeble remark has a strange power. It doesn't impinge on the reader's judgment or his freedom of choice. The author doesn't take one step toward him. He lets him make his own way, discover the marvel for himself and appraise it.

Am I wrong? It seems to me that Mérimée speaks of Beyle as Swann does of Odette de Crécy: "To think that I had my greatest love for a woman who didn't please me, *who wasn't my type!*" I would never dare claim that Mérimée was lying; but I can't believe that he and Stendhal agreed on only a very few subjects. Far from this, I think there existed between them a sort of unspoken agreement on everything, or at least on the viewpoint to be adopted for looking at the world, and that they argued only for the fun of it. Their ages, however, must not be discounted. When one is twenty-three, one can't know, one can't feel, one can't guess at everything, however subtle one is. Beyle was twenty years older than Mérimée, and what twenty years those were! Twenty years of Beylism and twenty years of the Empire. I suppose that Mérimée, when he in turn reached forty and had rid himself of the prejudices, obsessions, ready obstinacy and pusillanimity of a young genius, often thought of Beyle's ideas and ended by adopting them. He doesn't say that Stendhal was his master, because it wasn't in Stendhal's nature to play the master, nor in Mérimée's to tolerate one, but we can say it for him. Mérimée was a great and outstandingly original writer amid the "welter of nineteenth-century literature," but Stendhal's influence pervades everything he wrote and did. Besides, it would be very surprising for anyone who had met Stendhal at twenty-three and become his closest friend not to have been marked by it for life.

Stendhal's rise to fame so late in the day has considerably helped Mérimée's. The master was discovered only after his pupil, and people have grown used to taking the pupil for a master. One might almost say that Mérimée was a writer of the nineteenth century and Stendhal a writer of the twentieth.

17

For quite a time I suspected him of trying to be original. I ended by believing him to be perfectly sincere. Today, recalling all my memories, I am convinced that his eccentricities were completely natural and his paradoxes the usual result of the exaggeration into which contradiction imperceptibly leads one. Molière's Alceste is completely natural and sincere when, on being pressed to express some slight regrets for having been so hard on the verses of Oronte, he cries that "a man deserves to hang for having made them." Beyle's sallies were, in my opinion, simply the exaggerated expression of profound convictions.

I HAVE NEVER HEARD "experience" evoked except by elderly imbeciles who use this word to camouflage their capitulations, lack of spirit, inertia and even, on occasion, contemptible behavior. And yet there also exists a noble kind of experience. Mérimée here offers subtle and conclusive proof of it. This paragraph was written by a man in his fifties, who had had all of twenty or thirty years to develop a feeling for certain nuances. "I ended by believing . . . Today, recalling all my memories . . ." These phrases show that experience, in a gallant man, expresses itself with humility, the opposite of the moral cad who flaunts it as if it were a showy decoration.

At fifty, Mérimée had grasped the fact that Stendhal exaggerated because he had to make himself understood. He exaggerated in the same way as Rubens, who painted his figures larger than life but with perfect draftsmanship. To offer Rubens to people who like and understand only the engravings of Horace Vernet is asking to be sneered at. Fools take an infinite pleasure in criticizing Rubens; they regard this as showing a fine independence of judgment.

Mérimée's humility, which he is careful not to advertise, which the dear man expresses as coldly and discreetly as everything else, enchants me. Beyle did not misplace his friendship. If the reader will turn back to Paragraph 16, he will find there a significant sentence: "Apart from a few predilections and dislikes in literature, we had perhaps not a single idea in common . . ." That is all that is needed for two writers to understand each other and immediately recognize that they belong to the same family. I know, today, those colleagues with whom I get along and those with whom I don't. There are six or eight people who admire or loathe the same authors I do. That is enough for me to grow attached to them; I know what they think and how they think; I know the music that sounds in their hearts—the same echoes in mine. I would even say, almost without straining matters, that an identity of taste can take the place of everything else. It is less important to have monarchistic or republican ideas, to be a Jew or a Christian, an atheist or a believer (thus, I get along excellently with Stendhal and Péguy, Mérimée and Claudel, Diderot and Pascal, and *for the same reasons*), than it is to share the same principles regarding the use of the language, the way of elaborating one's thoughts, the degree of gaiety to give one's style. To make myself quite clear, one has every right, when one is Stendhal, to love Canova and revel in obscure debauches in the East End of London, but one has no right to like Victor Cousin or Villemain; in the same way today one has no right to like a certain pedantry in literature, a certain exaggerated humanitarianism, a certain demagogy and a certain sententiousness, all of which are currently in fashion. Among the famous writers of our time, I reckon there are eight or ten whom one couldn't possibly admire without being a hypocrite or an imbecile.

Intelligent young men are always on the alert for any exaggeration, and I can understand how Mérimée at first suspected Stendhal's true originality of being insincerity and felt his eccentricities to be contrived. At twenty he already had that inexorable and rather curt love of truth which was his great merit and his limitation all his life. To him the least extravagance seemed forced; at best, if he was well disposed, he consented to regard it as a game.

At forty, one realizes that a Stendhal doesn't play games, that he never plays them, for he hasn't the time. An extreme inner wealth, a host of original ideas, make one seem a rather odd sort of person. If Mérimée allowed this to deceive him, how must it have appeared to ordinary people? Alceste is a profound character, but when one is a very young man one appreciates only his comic or romantic aspects. Experience enables one to see beyond the comic or romantic surface; it opens up a doorway into the soul, which is neither funny nor sad but strange and enthralling, like a complex landscape.

Beyle's sallies were simply the exaggerated expression of profound convictions, because a great mind is all of one piece and expresses its philosophy in even the lightest of remarks, without seeing either malice or ridicule in them. Given a certain measure of wit, one sees the ridiculous side of people, behavior and things less and less as one acquires a greater insight into their causes. What strikes people as ridiculous is usually what they cannot explain; that is why fools frequently indulge in mockery—they see nothing but the surface and jeer only at appearances. Society wants nothing more; above all it demands on pain of contempt and hostility that one give it nothing more. If one speaks the truth when all that is required of one is light paradoxes, if one reveals the depth of things, even in the form of a joke, when all that is required of one is a superficial remark, one is simply branded as a bore, or pretentious, or eccentric. As a man of paradox, finally, for society invariably takes the truth, with its disconcerting glamour, for a paradox, and a paradox, with its shabby tinsel, for the truth. Society cannot conceive that a man of wit may not "take special pains" and that his sallies may be merely the comic extension, the extreme joking point of profoundly serious thoughts. The witticisms of a smart man about town depend on a special "turn of mind"; they are a succession of lucky hits, a series of little monuments in a desert. Those of a profound man resemble rather those delicate ridges that rise up out of the sea and are only the highest point of a reef which descends three hundred feet below the waves. Mérimée's dive lasted twenty years, but in twenty years he reached the foot of that Stendhalian rock whose existence he at first never even suspected.

I never knew where he got his opinions from on a subject over which he had the misfortune to find himself opposed to almost everyone else. What I learned of his early upbringing boils down to this one fact: that, when very young, he had been entrusted to the care of an old and surly ecclesiastic whose discipline left him with a feeling of resentment that never diminished. In truth, Beyle's mind revolted against all constraint and even all authority. One could win him over, and this was easy provided that one amused him; but to impose an opinion on him was impossible, for anyone who, in his dealings with him, assumed an air of superiority touched him on the raw. Forty years later he would still bitterly tell the story of how, when he tore a new coat at play, the abbé entrusted with his education rebuked him sharply for his misdemeanor before his comrades and told him that he was "a disgrace to religion and his family." Here is one of the exaggerations I spoke of just now. We used to laugh whenever Beyle told us this story; but he saw nothing in it but clerical tyranny and a horrible injustice, neither of them any laughing matter, and he still felt the wound inflicted on his young self-esteem as keenly as he had the day it happened.

I<small>T IS ODD</small> that Beyle should have told the Comte Gazul, his best friend, so little about his early upbringing, when he harps on it so often in his private writings, *Brulard* in particular. Without knowing the word "psychoanalysis," he was keenly aware of the importance of what one feels and sees at an early age. More than any other author except perhaps Rousseau, he strove hard to trace everything in his childhood which might have left a mark on his character. What Stendhalian doesn't know the charming passage in which he tells how his pretty mother sat athwart his bed and lit an incestuous fire in him? What Stendhalian doesn't know the ever present furies of this bourgeois childhood in Grenoble, Grandfather Gagnon, Aunt Séraphie, Chérubin Beyle and *espagnolisme?* It is not the purpose of this book to write literary history, so I shall pursue this no further. Besides, I have no learned discovery to add. I am not composing a postgraduate thesis, and this is the opposite of a scholarly handbook full of facts and dates. For anyone who is interested, there are biographies in plenty. M. Martineau tells all. As for me, I find biographies a bore. I am so incurious that I never question the three or four friends I have about the events that have marked their lives. The only things that interest me are the ways in which these events alter their hearts or minds.

Dates and dramatic highlights apart, Beyle's childhood fascinates me. I can sense its flavor at a distance of a hundred and sixty years; I can above all sense the retrospective judgment he passed on it in his fifties. The childhood of a superior man is a world of solitude. He spends his first fifteen to seventeen years in a complete desert, or, rather, in exile. He is a little Ovid among the Scythians. Those around him speak a language which is his, but which he doesn't understand, because the words are used to convey different meanings. And nobody understands him. They apply to him norms which suit every child but him. If he ingenuously expresses his daring ideas, he is scolded or laughed at. A child is a slave with no rights and every obligation. The superior child feels this slavery with special sharpness; he loathes the injustice of it. From the age of seven, he shuts himself up in a mental solitude, extremely fertile but painful at the time. As nothing prescribed for him suits him, he works out his own ideas and maxims for himself, singlehanded. At ten, the revolt is complete. This takes the form of a most vigorous hypocrisy and a great gift for lying, since he has to contrive some peace for himself. This personal education is excellent for the future. It forms indomitable hearts, which have early experienced the shock of the world and found the means to deaden it. Moreover, nothing is more salutary than a bad example. An intelligent boy brought up by idiots and accustomed to take the stand opposite theirs on every score will manage himself with wisdom and prudence and will never allow himself to wallow in those costly indulgences which waste so much time and energy.

Stendhal looked back on his childhood with a sort of loving horror. It weighed on him more than on anyone else. No one ever longed so intensely to emerge from that painful state; he yearned with all his heart for manhood and caught up with it as fast as he could. At eighteen, he was a sublieutenant of dragoons in the glorious army in Italy, which was drawn from the people and which was young. He had high boots and a big saber and talked like a seasoned old trooper. The Revolution had breathed on the bogies of his childhood in Grenoble. No regicide felt such pleasure as the little Henri Beyle when poor Louis XVI's head fell. He saw that they were beheading the bitter and suffocating monster of the old society, which lay crouched on his chest and was smothering him. They were beheading stupidity.

All children love upheavals, which are fun, annoy their parents and shut down schools. But how intoxicating when this upheaval is the work of youth, toppling over the old, setting up new ideas, proclaiming the triumph of intelligence over rancid stupidity and finally overthrowing the whole social system which was tying you down! The Revolution sent to the scaffold the idiots who had been held up to him as examples; what a revenge for a twelve-year-old boy exasperated by the stupidity and meanness of his family! The Revolution did much to appease the angry soul of Henry Brulard. He loved it madly, as he did the Empire, which gave the Revolution high boots.

The old and surly ecclesiastic of whom Mérimée writes was the famous Abbé Raillane, whose tyranny lasted for two years. There still exists a horrifying portrait of this character. With his hideous wig, his sparse and rectangular features like a Roman emperor steeped in vice, he resembles a sort of Tiberius in a cassock, at least so far as his expression, his cheekbones, his wrinkles and saurian eyes are concerned. Poor little Beyle, to have been subjected to such a rod of iron! I don't know whether the artist who engraved the portrait of the Abbé Raillane meant to make a caricature, but I don't believe he did. The abbé was a living anticlerical caricature, of the kind one sees today in the antireligious museums of Russia and which was enormously widespread in France in about 1900; they are so scurrilous that one can't help smiling over them. The Abbé Raillane was in truth the archetype of an ecclesiastical pedagogue. Stendhal himself couldn't have dreamed up a more frightful and at the same time conventional face. One can safely say that fate sent him his angels and devils with a sure hand.

To tell Beyle that he was "a disgrace to religion and his family" was typical of the Abbé Raillane's way. Such words go perfectly with the Tiberius face. They must have had a terrible ring to them. Certain grownups infallibly know, when necessary, how to make you feel like a little pariah, a little reprobate, how to cut you off with one word and for a futile reason from the general run of humankind in which children feel so at ease. I have known two ecclesiastics who were not as frightful as the Abbé Raillane but who made me hate religion when I was respectively eleven and twelve. There is a clerical spite and stupidity of which the bishops and superiors of seminaries should beware, for these unfailingly turn away from God all the more or less proud spirits that they single out for attack. Nor do I see any more to laugh at in the perfidies inflicted on me in my childhood by Monsignor B—— and the Abbé S—— than Stendhal did in the rebuke of the Abbé Raillane. These are grave matters; their consequences are infinite. Stendhal knew what had shaped him, what had bent his soul in one direction rather than another, what deserved to be treated lightly and what deserved to be taken seriously.

Childhood, even an unhappy one, always leaves sentimental and ironic memories. This was not so with Beyle—an additional proof of the originality of his feelings. The man he was at fifty carefully refrained from poking fun at the boy he had been; on the contrary, he admired this boy and looked up to him as a comrade in arms; he fully appreciated the battle fought by Henri Beyle for ten years against Chérubin, Séraphie, the whole town of Grenoble and the *ancien régime*, making the best of undependable allies like old Grandfather Gagnon, "a character *à la* Fontenelle"; he reveled in this boy's strength of spirit and capacity for solitude. The man of fifty remained true to the little boy. And how could one possibly treat these matters lightly? Such a heroic childhood fully deserved to inspire pride in the man who had lived through it. It would have been a mean trick to make a joke of it in order to amuse the company. The grief Stendhal felt over his mother's death when he was seven had no equal, other than the good this death did him in the long run. "The heart has either to break or to harden," says Chamfort. Beyle's began to harden at the age of seven. Those who have the luck and misfortune to lose their mothers so early benefit from an unusual step forward toward maturity. But a hard heart is not a heart of stone. Behind its armor plate it holds treasures of sensitivity and an ingenious capacity for suffering. An orphan who has never tormented his mother and never been exasperated by her brings an artlessness and bluntness into his love affairs; he isn't afraid to lapse back into solitude if he is jilted, but he also displays an overwhelming hunger for affection which sometimes makes him alarming. The motherless boy has an excessive virility which scares certain women and attracts others. I am convinced that Métilde Dembowski detected this excess of virility in Stendhal, despite his submissiveness, his shyness and his sexual failures, and that because of this she persistently refused to surrender to him and caused him an unhappiness which inspired songs and melodies as somber and heart-rending as those in Mozart's *Don Giovanni*.

"Beyle's mind revolted against all constraint and even all authority." Mérimée was here referring to the man of fifty, but he saw very clearly that this independent man of fifty was merely a continuation of the rebellious little boy. The only person in fifty-nine years who wielded any authority over Stendhal was Napoleon, and Stendhal didn't admire even him every day. So long as the Emperor ruled, he never gave way to imperial conformity, nor to adulation, nor to servility. Such are the benefits conferred by the spirit of contradiction. His sketch of Napoleon on the day of his coronation, his note of the "play-actor's smile," shows his freedom with regard to the idol. He admired Napoleon for what was admirable in him and because he was a "great soul," but he was a very cool judge of those sides of his character which revealed pettiness, spite or humbug. After Waterloo, Stendhal doubtless considered with good reason that there was nobody left in France or Italy with the necessary superiority to require his submission.

I can see how Stendhal was touched on the raw by those who sought to impose their opinions on him. Toward a man like him, who had excellent opinions of his own, this was the height of impertinence. For the roles must on no account be reversed: Stendhal's was precisely to make known his opinions, tested as they were by an infallible sensibility and a flawless intellect, and not to listen to the wavering and ephemeral opinions of others, the fruit of chance or circumstance.

The subject on which Stendhal "had the misfortune to find himself opposed to almost everyone else" was probably religion. The word "misfortune" is Mérimée's. For a man possessed by the spirit of contradiction, to find oneself opposed to almost everyone else is always a pleasure. To procure it, he will even go so far as to uphold things in which he doesn't believe. I don't, of course, pretend that Stendhal was not a sincere atheist. All the same, I cling to the notion that he overdid his atheism in order to scandalize the bigots.

19

"Our parents and masters," he used to say, "are our natural enemies when we come into the world." This was one of his aphorisms. Clearly, he didn't borrow his ideas from his tutors. He often quoted Helvétius with great admiration, and even made me read his book De l'Esprit; *but never, despite my requests, would he consent to reread it himself. I suppose that, among other opinions, he had taken that of the equality of human intellects from it. At least, he could never be persuaded that what appeared false to him might appear true to someone else. I believe he honestly imagined that at heart everyone shared his ideas but spoke a different language for reasons of self-interest, affectation, modishness or obstinacy. He was highly impious, an outrageous materialist or, to express it better, a personal enemy of Providence, perhaps as a result of the aphorism I have just quoted. He denied God and nevertheless resented Him as one resents a master. He never believed that a devout person could be sincere. I think that his long sojourn in Italy had contributed not a little to giving his mind that irreligious and aggressive twist which is so apparent in all his writings and for which he has been so castigated.*

THIS ANECDOTE about Helvétius, whom Stendhal forced Mérimée to read, is amusing. When had Stendhal read Helvétius himself? At fifteen, at sixteen? He saw him still through the eyes of that age, unless he had frankly forgotten him! The

92

books one read in one's youth play these tricks on one. One cherishes the same glorified memory of them as one does of the women with whom one first discovered love. At thirty one would barely turn to glance at the same beauties who seemed so divine when one was emerging from adolescence and whose possession one regarded as a priceless treasure. I never reread without a twinge of fear the books which enchanted me when I was twenty; I am afraid of finding them silly and of realizing that it was precisely this silliness which charmed me. Books are milestones which mark the various ages of the mind and permit one to measure its growth. There are some stages past which one honestly believes one has scorched at high speed, just as there are others to which one attaches an exaggerated importance. When Stendhal read Helvétius, the latter was still a subversive writer, an emancipator. He read him *against* his family, *against* Grenoble, the *ancien régime*, the clergy and so on, and hence with delight. As I have already said, it was in this way that, when I was thirteen or fourteen, I discovered Anatole France, who was forbidden me. These were the first books to give me a delight in sinning, and at the same time a feeling that I was committing, if I may put it this way, a *legitimate sin*. It was a sin only because it was forbidden, and I had placed myself outside these prohibitions.

In 1820, Helvétius no longer emancipated anyone. He was a bore. Stendhal, who refused to reread him, was to some extent aware of this. The Revolution and the Empire did the greatest harm to the intrepid philosophers of the eighteenth century: they made them insipid. So many social, moral, political and even metaphysical upheavals, so many armies, conquests, massacres and enthusiasms cast Baron d'Holbach and his friends into the gray waters of Lethe. The philosophers of the eighteenth century, even Voltaire, even Rousseau, appear to me like so many little Moseses arrested by death before the flood of the Revolution, men of the old world in spite of their ideas, unworthy of attaining the promised land of liberty and the rights of man.

The equality of human intellects is one of those ideas philosophers love: true in principle or in the absolute sense, but false in the practice of life, or the contingent, one of those ideas which, when they meet them, enchant young men of intelligence but of no adult experience. One always retains something of the ideas with which one was enamored in one's youth, even if one has subsequently proved their weakness a thousand times over. At sixteen, Beyle was without illusions, without hypocrisy, completely honest with himself and probably without imagination, all of which inclines one toward truth and a blunt way of expressing oneself. For people of no imagination, who are nevertheless honest and shrewd, truth has a prodigious advantage over falsehood. It exists. It is there. It stares you in the face. It fills the world with wonderful revelations to be discovered and handed on. Beside it, everything else seems insipid, particularly the inventions of the poets, which are often mere exercises in rhetoric. Every young writer without imagination has dreamed of producing a vast tome containing nothing but himself, seen through a magnifying glass or a microscope, which would make up a complete portrait of man. Whence so many private diaries. Beyle at sixteen, an explorer of truth, happy each time he "caught it in the act," madly in love with its bitter taste, charmed by its harshness, enchanted by its dissonances, thrilled to note that it was always in disagreement with the conventions and shibboleths of those around him, discovering with intoxication its cynical or brutal laws, saw an entirely new world taking shape before him, which had been carefully concealed from him during his childhood—a world full of dazzling colors and clear lines, devoid of affectation and exaggeration. Such a spectacle is enthralling. It drives one to wild enthusiasm. It pulverizes discretion and prudence. One is dazed by one's discoveries. One cannot keep them to oneself. One appoints oneself the herald of truth, one ingenuously sings its praises, one aggressively proclaims it. The force of the obvious is so great for those endowed with the eyes to see it that it blinds them to everything else. This rare faculty, instead of making them conceited, makes them modest. They can't conceive that not everyone possesses it. They can't imagine they are dealing with myopics and not with hypocrites. That is where the beautiful theory of the equality of human intellects according to Helvétius falls down. It fails to take into account the fact that the earth is filled with shortsighted people. Truth is an absolute, like beauty, but the absolute demands an eagle eye.

I don't know if any psychoanalyst has pondered over Beyle's case. When I think of the fat, comic volume devoted by Mme. Marie Bonaparte to Edgar Allan Poe, I sincerely hope not. Yet Beyle would furnish material for a *serious* and perhaps fruitful psychoanalytical study. The ways in which his childhood impinged on his heart and mind were legion, and the earnestness with which he studied them shows the importance he attached to them. The aphorism that parents and masters are our natural enemies is not entirely natural coming from a man of forty or fifty. Making due allowances for exaggeration and the pleasure to be had from stating an unconventional idea, it must above all be attributed to the cruel memories of a child prodigy kept for a long time in leading strings by second-rate teachers, misunderstood and bound hand and foot by lies and conventions which he had seen for what they were and which horrified him. Hostility between people who are not of "the same breed" is fatal. By this I mean spiritual breed, naturally. The inferior breed always exerts all its strength against the

superior and reduces it to the most abject slavery.* Grownups
are exasperated in every possible way by a little slave who
doesn't recognize the same principles they do. Their one idea
is to bring him to heel, to *break* him. They want to make
him like themselves. This attempt is violently resented by superior children, and they resist it with all their might. Victoriously, on the whole. But they drag after them the fatigues of
these early battles all their lives, in the form of sexual failures, blunders or fits of violence.† I know masses of commonplace children who live on the best terms in the world with
their parents and masters; old and young love each other
dearly and to their mutual delight.

It is difficult for me to speak of Stendhal's irreligion. I would
probably have analyzed it very well ten years ago, but I understand this feeling less and less, perhaps because, contrary
to my hero, I live in a world without religion. The irreligion
toward which the spirit of contradiction so strongly impelled
him is something I flee from under the influence of that same
spirit. The spectacle of Italy, which, God knows, is almost
calculated to make one ungodly, hasn't been enough to throw
me back into outrageous materialism, any more than has that
of the Puritan humbugs of England and America. A friendship
with God, which I had long denied myself, reconciled me with
myself when I was about thirty-five. From this I draw no conclusions as to the existence or nonexistence of God. I simply
know that this reconciliation has brought me a happiness I
didn't possess before. This, to my mind, is sufficient, and I am

---

* "From that moment my vocation was decided: to live in Paris and write
comedies like Molière. This was my one obsession, which I hid under the
deepest dissimulation; Séraphie's tyranny had given me the habits of a
slave." (*Brulard*, Chapter 16.)

† On December 4, 1835, Stendhal, aged fifty-two, refused a willing lady
because his conquest's aquiline nose reminded him of the nose of the
Abbé Raillane. Even so, the lady was "agreeable and pretty." But her nose
would have provoked a fiasco.

quite unconcerned if I pass for a chickenhearted philosopher. These matters are too important to be subordinated to considerations of respectability. I consider any man an idiot who rejects a worth-while happiness out of regard for public opinion or out of fidelity to intellectual principles which are no more demonstrable than their opposites. I should add that atheism must not be mistaken for anticlericalism. The clergy know very well how to foster this confusion.

The irreligious and aggressive twist in Stendhal's books comes straight from Voltaire. It is an amusing tradition, to which I myself yielded a little, for the fun of it, in the old days. But the field is limited, and one condemns oneself to repeating the same things in the same tone. This has become stereotyped, to my mind. And who would "castigate" one for it today? There is no longer any merit in being ungodly. On the contrary, when I happen to write pleasant things about God there are always critics ready to laugh at me and reproach me for having one eye on the Académie. I think that, had his atheism been a little less castigated, Stendhal would have shown himself a little less persistent in his ungodliness. But how could he have adopted the bigotry or sentimental religiosity of the first half of the nineteenth century without vomiting? Not to mention that one spurs oneself on by writing, one wants to be more and more provocative, to prove oneself more and more indomitable. I have been through that myself.

20 *M. Sainte-Beuve, with his customary sagacity, has drawn attention to one of the most striking features of Beyle's character: fear of being made a dupe, and a constant concern to protect himself from this misfortune. Hence that artificial callousness, that desperate analysis of base motives for every generous action, that resistance to the impulses of the heart—all much more affected than real with him, or so it seems to me. The dislike and contempt he had for false sensibility often made him go to the other extreme, to the horror of those who, not knowing him intimately, took what he said about himself literally. Not only did he attach no importance to correcting the more or less spiteful interpretations people gave to what he said or wrote, but he also took a sly delight—born of vanity, I think —in passing for a monster of immorality in most people's eyes. He has said, in one or another of his prefaces, "I write for only about twenty people, whom I have never seen but who, I hope, understand me . . ."*

Mérimée, or the master of concise prose. This man says everything with a desperate economy, and it is sometimes hard to paraphrase him. When he leaves room for ambiguity (and I detect it here in "more affected than real with him, *or so it seems to me*") one is never sure that it isn't simply an understatement, a piece of politeness or a sign of modesty.

What is one to think of the "sagacity" of M. Sainte-Beuve?

It can, alas, hardly be denied! But this sagacity applied far more in small things than in big ones. His article on Stendhal, to which Mérimée alludes, is a blend of truth as regards details and error as regards the whole, very typical of his manner. As always, arrogance—for he sincerely believed himself to be the leading writer of his century—led Sainte-Beuve into petty spite. His great contemporaries embarrassed him. Half in rage, half in good faith, he revenged himself by denigrating them, thinking no doubt that posterity would take his word for it. To accuse Balzac, in writing the sublime *Lys dans la vallée*, of having plagiarized the appalling *Volupté*,* to accuse him of this secretly in private papers, is less a proof of sagacity than one of blind vanity.

Few books have made such a frightful impression on me as Sainte-Beuve's private notebooks, which have been published under the title *Mes Poisons*. I am not, I think, in any way prejudiced; I can read the worst horrors without a shiver, and some of them have even diverted me, such as the Marquis de Sade, who remains consistently jovial amidst his hecatombs; but these *Poisons* sent a cold shudder down my spine; by the time I had finished them I felt really soiled. The soul whose portrait they furnish is so abject that one can't even bring oneself to admire its prodigious sincerity, which generally leads one to forgive the vilest and basest deeds in the name of art, or the intellect. Certain emotions are truly *inadmissible* on account of their baseness, for no confession, unless dictated by repentance, is made without complacency. Sainte-Beuve's smugness over his vices is insufferable; there is something diabolical about it; he describes them with the same loving objectivity as trees, flowers or familiar faces. He lives completely at ease in their company, without making the slightest effort to

---

* A novel by Sainte-Beuve.—TR.

rid himself of them. Such an acceptance of self seems to me monstrous. Here is an atheism far more complete, if not as provocative, as Beyle's.

Beyle's uprightness, nobility, delicacy and punctilious sense of honor have absolutely nothing in common with the profound vulgarity of Sainte-Beuve. He is a lion judged by a serpent. The perfection of the lion is incomprehensible to the serpent. The serpent regards the lion from afar, pokes fun at his ways and outlines his idiosyncrasies, but none of this ever penetrates to his soul. Who would guess from reading Sainte-Beuve that Stendhal was anything but an agreeable companion, always a gentleman, and an essayist of note who, rather late in life, made the mistake of trying to write novels? To pick on his fear of being made a dupe is a typical piece of shrewdness on Sainte-Beuve's part, a just observation inserted into a general judgment which is most unjust.

This fear of being gullible, this artificial callousness, desperate analysis of base motives, resistance to the impulses of his heart and dislike of false sensibility which made him go to the other extreme merely reflect the spirit of contradiction. Mérimée knew Stendhal during the Restoration, which is to say in a society aping that of the *ancien régime*. At forty, Stendhal found himself once again immersed in the provincial life, the hypocrisy, triviality and prejudices he so hated. But now he was forty. For twenty years he had joyously employed the manners of the Revolution and the Grande Armée: a ready cynicism, dirty jokes, licentiousness and an all-conquering good humor. These permanently mark any man's character. In 1820 he was a hussar among bigots. Back in Paris, he found himself again confronted by the ideas and customs of Grenoble, but with the strength of a man of forty, with a richer and simpler mind and heart. Now he took his revenge. He revealed himself in a way he had been unable to do in 1788, under the despotic rule of Chérubin Beyle. The conduct that Mérimée describes here has been summed up in a phrase Saint-Simon reports Louis XIV as having coined to describe Philippe d'Orléans: "a flaunter of vices." It is next to impossible for any warm-blooded and self-respecting man not to be a flaunter of vices when he is plunged into hypocrisy, conformity, discretion, circumspection, conventional ideas and authorized thoughts. The appearances of virtue, when they do not mask true virtue, force the latter in a way to misrepresent itself and camouflage itself by depravity. There must be a contrast. True virtue never suffers from having the same face as the false. An additional advantage: imbeciles always fail to detect it.

Self-misrepresentation is the great temptation of noble souls. Some acquire an astonishing skill at it. We have a striking example of it today in M. Jean Paulhan, who has misrepresented himself for nearly forty years, but who has, with time, managed to come by half a dozen faithful friends who no longer believe anything he says about himself.

I once wrote, in a work of my youth, that it is better to be the dupe of others than of oneself, but this doesn't apply to Stendhal, for he was the very opposite of a self-deceiver. It was his spirit of contradiction, enhanced by a savage modesty, that led him to be offensive in conversation and made him appear ill-mannered, just as it drove him to constant irony with regard to the nobler features of the characters in his novels. But no one is taken in by any of this. As one reads him, one sees an extreme tenderness underlying all his sarcasms. Mérimée, who had heard him put forward a thousand subversive arguments in tones of the highest mockery, must have been less conscious of it than we, the posthumous readers of *Le Rouge et le Noir* and *La Chartreuse*, that band of about twenty people who understand him.

21 For him, there were only two kinds of people in the world: those whose company he enjoyed and those by whom he was bored. To make the smallest sacrifice, to take the slightest trouble to win the esteem or affection of the latter was to expose himself to relations which to him were intolerable. Beyle's independent or, if you like, vagabond spirit rejected every form of constraint. Anything that impaired his freedom was odious, and I am not altogether sure that he made a very clear distinction between the tedious and the pernicious. His constant eagerness to penetrate all the mysteries of the human heart sometimes even drew him to people for whom he felt little esteem. "But," he used to say, "at least with them there is something to be learned." Besides, his proud and loyal spirit, incapable of any meanness, alienated him from such company directly he found in it some advantage other than satisfaction of his curiosity.

His judgments on men and things were most often dictated by memories of the boredom or pleasure he had had from them. He couldn't endure boredom and shared the opinion of the physicians who authorized the Duc de Lauraguais to take legal proceedings against a bore for attempted homicide. There was no kind of exaggeration to which his bad temper didn't prompt him against books or people who had had the misfortune to make him yawn.

FOR ME, there are two kinds of tedium: the sterile kind, which comes from outside, and the fruitful kind, which one experiences in solitude, the acedia felt by the hermits in the Thebaic desert, when one's thoughts fly off in a whirlwind, when one's heart and soul relax and reform themselves like fallow soil. This second type of tedium has marvelous moments of intoxication, exaltation and brilliance. Creative people know it well and cultivate it. They welcome it gladly. They prefer it to all other distractions. The transition from such tedium to inspiration is imperceptible; it forms the cement of great works.

Ordinary people find it hard to understand the steadfastness of Victor Hugo, who remained eighteen years on his island. Yet it is quite simple: this great man, like his fellows, delighted in boredom. Or, if you prefer it, he was "sufficient unto himself." According to a formula of the mystic St. John of the Cross, he made solitude "resonant." In this solitude, he discovered himself and drew on all the potentialities of his genius. For those who like boredom, nothing is more tedious than any form of diversion. For them it provides nothing but a discouraging spectacle of vanity or stupidity. The Hugo family seethed with impatience on Jersey and Guernsey, pouncing on the least excuse to rush off to Brussels, London or even Paris in pursuit of amusement. Victor himself never budged. For eighteen years he remained in a *tête-à-tête* with himself, with the ocean and sometimes, if he is to be believed, with God. What an example! And incomprehensible, even to those closest to him. One gets the tedium one deserves. The kind which is distilled in solitude by a noble spirit like Hugo's and which gives rise to a gigantic series of works is worth the gayest and subtlest distractions.

The tedium one encounters in society or in books is of

quite another order. It leaps out on you like an assassin. It kills you for one, two, three or four hours. It snatches a moment out of your brief life and throws it on the rubbish heap. One goes out in quest of pleasure and finds death. There are the seeds of a little drama here. Anyone who is conscious of the fleetingness of time, of the brevity of life and the need to enjoy it as fully as possible before final extinction, feels blind panic and fury before this brigand. It is a question of defending one's very life. I really cannot see why Stendhal should have made "the smallest sacrifice" or taken "the slightest trouble to win the esteem or affection" of people by whom he was bored. Because they were powerful, perhaps, and might have helped his career? He had elected, since Waterloo, to thumb his nose at promotion. Since birth, his vocation had chosen for him a profession in which there is no promotion, in which no favor obtained at the cost of yawns or sycophancy brings even one degree of progress. Why should he seek boredom when his one and only ambition was simply to earn the wherewithal to be able to write? Stendhal conceded what little was necessary to boredom in order to wangle his post as consul at Civitavecchia and to keep it. Once one has decided to lead an independent and impecunious existence, and provided that one sticks to this choice, there is no longer the faintest reason for seeking to please people who annihilate one. On the contrary, they must be permanently discouraged right from the start. I have always looked on Montherlant's hero, Costals, who divides his life between writing and women, as a wise man of great magnitude. It seems to me that this man, who devotes himself more or less to the only two occupations that he cares about and that he holds to be essential, can never have been bored.

One word stands out in what Mérimée says: "Beyle's independent or, if you like, *vagabond* spirit." We can bet that when he was bored he thought nostalgically of all the delights he was missing on this account. His powerful imagination conjured up detailed pictures of the pretty woman he wouldn't meet, the unique opportunities for happiness taking place a hundred yards away, perhaps, that he would never know. Such is the martyrdom of independent or vagabond spirits. They ceaselessly and nostalgically imagine the things they don't have and are always afraid to tie themselves down. Independence is often just a vague but consuming desire for the charms of the unknown. Hence a propensity for vagabondage. Stendhal regarded bores as obstacles that stood between him and happiness. Whence his hatred, his exaggerations, and so on. Independent people, in love with liberty, wish to be constantly unfettered, free to change their minds at any moment and to follow unexpected paths without constraint. When they are with a bore, they have a horrible feeling of being trapped. They feel entitled to any act of violence, provided that it permits them to return to their captivating saunter through life, when the most intriguing adventures are possible, when boredom at least becomes solitary again.

Stendhal's penchant for low company, over which Mérimée casts a veil for reasons of modesty, reveals a natural spirit of daring. Great artists love eccentricity and unfamiliar surroundings. Stendhal knew what stuff his soul was made of; there was hardly any danger that his shady connections would drag him down into a life of crime or dishonesty! Did Fabre begin to hop or buzz as a result of his study of insects? The same applies to Stendhal and the obscure friends with whom he went on orgies, or the detestable Baron de Mareste, who combined all the faults of the profligate Louis XV and the bourgeois Louis Philippe.

To hate boredom and forgive everyone who amuses you is to value life at its true worth and avoid falling into the lethal prejudice of rancor, vengeance, false self-respect and the illusory respect of boredom. A sizable dose of wit or charm was already necessary to amuse a man like Stendhal. I conclude that, all things considered, amusement is an effective touchstone of friendship.

Imaginative and impulsive though he was, Beyle nevertheless firmly maintained that he always acted according to reason and obeyed the rules of logic. This word "logic" often cropped up in his conversation, and his friends will remember the particular emphasis with which he pronounced it—slowly and separating the two syllables with a comma: "Lo,gic." Logic must always be our guide in all our actions; but his was not of the usual type, and one was sometimes hard put to it to follow the thread of his reasoning. I remember how one day we wanted to write a play together in which the hero felt remorse for a crime he had committed. "To rid oneself of remorse, what does Lo-gic say?" He thought for a moment. "We must found a school of mutual instruction." Our play progressed no further.

HERE I find Mérimée flagrantly guilty of shadow thinking. Stendhal's reply is luminous. It seems obscure only because it leaves out the reasoning that led up to it and which may be reconstructed as follows: Remorse is not a natural feeling, since there are periods when crime does not inspire it, crimes condemned today which were considered lawful two centuries ago, and, finally, men on whom crimes weigh no more heavily than a sneeze. Remorse is therefore the artificial product of a certain moral code. To suppress it, one has only to construct a different moral code, whose precepts will exclude it. The school of mutual instruction resembles the "Society of the Friends of Crime" whose statutes the Marquis de Sade so amusingly gives in his *Juliette* (which Beyle had read), a club of unprincipled and relentless scoundrels in whom the idea of remorse would merely have raised a guffaw.

Perhaps Stendhal's reply was just a piece of flippancy intended to show that he didn't take the project of collaborating on a play really seriously. But the flippancies of witty men are more profound than many sound arguments; they provide more grounds for reflection.

It is not surprising that Beyle, who was all imagination and impulse, should constantly refer to logic. In this way his head tried to effect a balance with his heart. In this way he battled with himself. In this way he put himself off the scent. I have mentioned earlier the contradiction of Don Juan versus the man of sensibility. This second contradiction is exactly the same. What one wants to be always seems finer than what one is. Nothing seemed finer to Stendhal, a man of imagination, than to pass for a cold man of logic. But, knowing himself inside out, he gave his demonstrations of logic a professorial and comic guise which undermined much of its serious nature.

The Baron de Mareste, a character totally devoid of spontaneity, logical down to the pettiest detail, finally earned his dislike. On the other hand, he showed to his dying breath an extreme tenderness for slightly mad characters, Italian for preference.

I am surprised that Mérimée does not stress how French Stendhal was in character, so addicted to logic and at the same time incapable of applying it in his life (for his writings are filled with true logic). The world-wide reputation the French have acquired for being a logical people is certainly calculated to arouse suspicion. Our nation is no more logical than any other; it only prides itself on being so. I don't know a single Frenchman, either intelligent or stupid (the stupid ones are perhaps more rabid on this score) who doesn't invoke logic in every possible connection. "You must do that; it's logical!" or "Why do that? It's not logical!" I have heard such remarks a thousand times over in every class of French society. Laborers pronounce them as readily as bankers, schoolmasters or ministers, and in the same tone of voice. In France the inexpiable sin, the sin against the Holy Ghost, is illogicality. Logic being the instrument of the thinker, one measures thereby the respect in which we hold philosophy.

He used to say that on entering life a man should have his ready-made provision of maxims for the mishaps that most ordinarily befall him. Once he has adopted these, they must no longer be disputed; it is enough to rapidly consider whether the case in point over which one is perplexed can be solved by one of the general precepts one has stored away. "Never pardon a lie," "Seize by the hair your first opportunity for a duel on going out into the world," "Never repent of any foolish action or remark"—these were some of his maxims.

I HAVE SEEN many unhappy people; I have been unhappy myself. Whether it had to do with myself or with others, I have always noticed that adversity has a hard edge only when one passively submits to it. Directly one opposes it with some action, directly one mobilizes oneself, takes decisions, goes to war against it, the unhappiness is dispelled and sorrow takes flight. There are still difficulties ahead, of course—setbacks and defeats—but these don't wear down one's spirit as they did before. One is no longer an object; one is no longer a slave to fate, content to moan unprofitably in one's chains; one passes into the state of being a subject. If, when it comes down to it, my will is not the stronger, at least I shall have made use of it; and if it hasn't triumphed over events, at least it will have modified them, deflected them a little; at least it will have deadened their shock. You are never completely conquered if you have defended yourself well, and you can still hope to be the victor the next time. Such thoughts are quite enough to make you very gay.

Stendhal's maxims are those of a man who has *thought about life* and thought modestly, not as an empty philosopher but as an active, practical and wise man. This is also like a mathematician, who is fond of having theorems. I love this idea of forging maxims for oneself. Behind it I see an ingenuous mind, a man who knows that his first impulses are not often the right ones and who has suffered abominably from a maddening *esprit de l'escalier*, or afterwit, which whispers the correct attitude to take or the right words to say five minutes or twenty-four hours too late. Stendhal, like every great writer, must have felt ill at ease when it came to extemporizing and must have been capable of salty, biting, apt repartee only when holding his pen in the silence of his study. Brilliant and witty though he was, his sensitive soul must have sometimes left him stranded in society, before some piece of boorishness or rather too overt an insult. It was at such moments that maxims came to the rescue, moments when his heart and head suddenly emptied under the effect of indignation or shame. Cold, soulless people have no need of maxims. From childhood on they obey *rules,* which for them take the place of character. When one doesn't know the rules, when one trusts to one's instinct, when one mars no pleasure by pausing to reflect, when one is unconcerned over one's attitude, one experiences many tricky moments in which maxims are extremely useful.

A man without maxims is a state without a policy, and a bad maxim is preferable to no maxim at all. Having maxims gains one time, abolishes indecision and gives life a determined aspect which paves the way for happiness more readily than anything else. A man with maxims is a man armed, and he wins respect. The three maxims quoted by Mérimée are irreproachable, for they each recommend a choice of the most difficult attitude. For undecided minds, difficulty should always be the criterion. There are few choices whose terms are equal; if one doesn't know which path to follow, one must embark on the most arduous, the one that climbs and that demands fatigue. Through practice, one comes to see that the "difficult solutions" are the best, even if one has to expend a great deal of energy to achieve them.

To return to Stendhal's maxims, nothing is easier than to condone a lie: a little negligence or optimism is enough. To believe that a liar will grow truthful is a convenient excuse for doing nothing. It permits one to sleep with an easy conscience, untroubled by bad dreams. Certain people sleep all their lives; no perfidy ever succeeds in opening their eyes. They pass for indulgent when they are indolent or indifferent, or selfish. They are, above all, eternal dupes—people who must set little store by life to accept the fact that the truth is concealed from them so easily. To condone a lie is to make oneself an accessory to the sin of lying. It is, in a sense, being a hypocrite.

When one is very young, it is the easiest thing in the world to allow opportunities for a duel to slip by. This is not exactly cowardice, but at most prudence or even uncertainty; an insult can sometimes be subtle, and great is the temptation to decide that it isn't one after all.

Finally, it is extremely easy to repent of a foolish word or deed, and to poison one's heart over it for a week. True strength of character lies in extirpating the folly from one's soul, in burning it out like a wart, declaring it null and void and determining that one is absolutely identical with what one was before. Why shouldn't one amputate an act of folly, just as the wolf bites off a paw when it is caught in a trap?

I suppose that, besides these three maxims, Stendhal had forged himself a hundred others, all equally proud, and that this sort of private *Discours de la Méthode* was precious to him, provided that he acted on it. But he did act on it, let there be no doubt as to that. This is proved by what Mérimée and society called his "eccentricities," which were simply the strict application of wise precepts. What a lesson in modesty! Stendhal, a writer of genius and a staggering psychologist, didn't trust his instinct to guide him!

Although he was never very bold with women, he preached temerity to the young. "One succeeds," he often said, "once in ten times. Let us say once in twenty. Isn't the chance of being happy once worth the risk of nineteen snubs, and even of being held up to ridicule nineteen times?"

BEYLE at fifty had the same attitude to women as Cherubino. The mere word "woman" was enough to arouse him, to delight him. "A girl, a woman, ah, what sweet names are those! How distracting they are!" Women's bodies, silken smooth, different, beguiling, offered him joys which he never wearied of imagining and which, in thought, seemed to him fabulous. A book was written not so long ago which strove to prove that Beyle was a pederast—and a police spy into the bargain. Nothing could be more absurd. To call him a police spy shows a complete failure to understand his heart; to call him a pederast is to show complete ignorance of his body. I think I know my Beyle at least as well as the authors of the book in question, and I cannot find the faintest trace of spying or of homosexuality. On the contrary, the most supercilious honor, an honor in the Spanish (or Calabrian) manner, the honor of a Carbonaro who would brave the Spielberg* and the rack rather than betray the names of his comrades. A masculine temperament of the most decided kind, and of a man little

---

* The prison into which the Austrians threw Italian nationalists.—Tr.

pursued but constantly pursuing, constantly lying in wait with his heart on the alert, seeing "promises of happiness" in the face of every pretty woman.

Beyle was certainly unlucky in love, and far more so than Guillaume Apollinaire, for he was shy, ugly and had a wit so sharp that it could be brutal. A real and dazzling wit that constantly verges on cynicism frightens pretty women. They feel they will be unable to dominate it, and their pride gets the better of any potential inclination. Promises of happiness in pretty faces don't appear to those who know how to read them. Apollinaire was big, fat, jovial, resplendent with poetry and licentiousness. He seduced young girls in railway carriages in a twinkling. He was a well-fed Apollo disguised as a lieutenant of artillery in the French Army. Beyle was more like Vulcan, but with the profound gaze of Mercury.

At fourteen, under the magnificent chestnut trees in the public gardens of Grenoble, madly in love with Mlle. Kably, to whom he never spoke a single word, he perceived that love causes a burn and that this burn is terrible. By the time he was fifty-nine, after having been burned an incalculable number of times, his heart was seamed with scars but quite unhardened for all that, and he felt the same lurches of fear as he had at fourteen. How idiotic to maintain that he was a pederast! Had he been, he would have said so in *Brulard*, or in his *Journal* or somewhere else. He would have noted it without any particular sense of pride, simply as one aspect of his nature. This man devoid of prejudice must have thought that it was no very grave matter to be a pederast, that it was quite unimportant and concerned nobody but oneself, and anyway that each man makes his own salvation as best he can. In his private writings, so far as the heart and emotions are concerned, we find nothing but women. Ugly, pretty, even poor Miss Appleby, scrawny and badly dressed—they all inspire desire. There can be no mistaking the tastes of the man who discusses them.

Beyle doubtless hadn't "a way with women" and so was not run after by them; but he ran after them eagerly himself. When he says that he set out every morning in pursuit of happiness, he meant above all that he set out in pursuit of women. The slightest amorous adventure smacks of love with a man like Beyle, who couldn't avoid putting a hint of rapture into everything he undertook. Besides, he was the opposite of a well-satisfied man, and the prospect of discovering an unknown body, of holding it in his arms and taking it, made him swoon in anticipation. This rare happiness, rarely attained, is immensely precious.

People like to say that women choose men, and that the latter are more often seduced than seducers. Beyle, ugly, shy and a hunter, was very male in that he himself sought to do the seducing. He was generally an unlucky seducer, but he always desired, he was never passive like the handsome young men that women take up with or steal from each other without, so to speak, asking their advice, and to whom they are attracted just because of their indifference as men who are loved. For the hunter, the woman is a *prey*. This idea of a prey adds greatly to love. The man who is chosen has less pleasure than the man who takes possession. Beyle, with his prodigious interest in and ceaseless advances to them, put women on their guard. A woman grants her favors less easily to the man who appears to attach an enormous price to them than to the man who cares nothing or acts as if he cares nothing for them.

Stendhal's argument regarding boldness in love strikes one by its mathematical precision. Who would deny that happiness, or even just a possibility of it, is worth nineteen snubs? No serious-minded person, certainly; that is to say, no one who doesn't set vanity or respectability above happiness. But to receive nineteen snubs is an ordeal worthy of the great romances of chivalry. One has to be truly unlucky in love to endure it without flinching.

He laughed at me when he saw me study-ing Greek at twenty. "You are on the battlefield," he said. "This is no longer the moment to polish your rifle; you must fire."

MY GOD, how I understand Stendhal's hatred of childhood! At eighteen, I had but one desire, cherished since I was ten: to escape from that frightful state, in which one has no respon-sibility, no freedom, no strength, countless duties and the per-petual obligation to lie. Looking back, my childhood seems an interminable period of dismal boredom and constraint. I felt a stranger to everybody, both family and friends. With the lat-ter the only thing I had in common was a taste for high jinks or wild laughter. I was as dishonest with them as with my fam-ily. To these last, I showed myself in the light of a docile little boy: I never argued, I carefully concealed my thoughts, my desires and the books I read. To my friends I acted the know-all, the freethinker; I hid equally from them my true thoughts, my true desires and the books I read.

At nineteen, I had my first taste of freedom, an intoxicating discovery which was very prejudicial to my studies. The boys and girls around me, on the other hand, pursued their studies with enthusiasm. They clung to their childhood like puppies about to be drowned; they relived it and nostalgically evoked its charms and past delights. They went to the university as they had gone to the *lycée*, obediently, and returned home to their worthy parents. They prolonged their childhood beyond the permitted bounds. Their pusillanimity exasperated me. I found them insipid in their thirst for knowledge. They turned up their noses at a thousand thrilling adventures within arm's reach for the benefit of a pointless degree or a ridiculous diploma. A year later (in 1940) I had the luck to be called up, to fight for a fortnight, to be a prisoner for two months and then to escape. I cared little for study; those two and a half months of real life put me off it forever. For two and a half months I had, to quote Stendhal, fired my rifle. To revert to polishing it struck me as stupid past belief and quite beyond my powers. Back from the war, I found again my comrades, who were still polishing, who would continue to polish until they were thirty, until they retired. After which, they would hang their glittering weapons on the rack. The sight of this nauseated me and threw me back into the pursuit of adventure, toward which I was already drawn by the wish to lead a life totally different from the one that had been my lot during my youth, and by the hope of setting myself above my family through my exploits.

I remember, when I was twelve, how irritated I was whenever I was told that this was the best time of life and that I would never be so happy again. To begin with, it wasn't true: I am immeasurably happier today, at thirty-eight, than I was then, in spite of taxation, the burden of a family, the need to make decisions, and so on; I do what I please, I see whom I like and, in however small a way, I influence the course of history. Apart from which I enjoy responsibilities; at twelve I suffered from not having any. Come to that, I suffered from everything, and principally from never being able to give my opinion, which was always in complete disagreement with the prejudices, precepts and moral code of the grownups.

Today, I am always exasperated when I read those countless novels, the horrible posterity of the absurd *Grand Meaulnes*, in which our contemporary authors apply themselves to depicting, transposed to a greater or lesser degree, the captivating charms of their childhood, their ecstatic discovery of love or nature, and so forth. Never has the prejudice in favor of "childhood, that golden age" been so rife. My God, what can those authors have been like as children? What little domestic animals, what arrant puppies stuffed with food, always ready to lick the master's hand in return for a lump of sugar.

There are some castrated or stupid nations which settle down quite comfortably under a despotic government that metes out to them a certain level of material prosperity and tell themselves they are happy because they eat well. The price of happy childhood is usually only cowardice and stupidity. The average educator is a terrible despot, kind, sometimes generous, but permitting only the dullest conformity. In my childhood I knew dozens of little boys who used to repeat the idiotic sayings of their parents with feigned or sincere admiration. Their hypocrisy or stupidity put me in a rage. What child hasn't been guilty a hundred times over of slavish approval of his natural masters, when everything within him instinctively and intellectually condemns the ineptitudes being hammered into him? That is the most appalling and characteristic vice of the slave, and its punishment is inevitable: in a few years' time the slave becomes as stupid as his master.

Beyle's childhood, *outwardly*, doesn't seem to have been unhappy. He belonged to a well-to-do family; he was "the grandson of Monsieur Gagnon," which meant something in Grenoble in 1794; he was well housed, well fed, well dressed; he was given a good education. But seen from within, seen through his eyes, even forty years later, it was the gloomiest childhood imaginable. A varied succession of bruises, wounds, hypocrisies, revolts and hatreds. An intolerable state of moral subjection. Oh, let manhood come as quickly as possible! Henri's device was that of the soldiers of the second year of

the Republic: "Liberty or death!" This led to his becoming a
sublieutenant of dragoons at seventeen, with the army in Italy.
Here was one boy who didn't polish his rifle for very long. But
the reward of superior children is that Providence gives them
a rifle when they are twelve or thirteen and makes snipers of
them.

26

After the maxims came the recipes, which he supplied fully guaranteed. Some of these I remember. One of the main causes of our torments is self-consciousness. For a young man, it is quite an undertaking to enter a salon. He imagines that everyone is staring at him and nearly dies of fright lest there should be something about his dress or bearing which isn't absolutely irreproachable. One of our friends used to suffer inordinately from this timidity, and Beyle used to say of him that when he came into Mme. Pasta's salon one always had the feeling that he had broken a piece of china in the anteroom. "I recommend to you the recipe I used to follow," he told him. "Go in with the attitude that chance has led you to adopt on the stairs; it matters little whether it is suitable or not; be like the statue of the Commendatore and do not alter your demeanor until the excitement of making your entrance has completely died away."

Does anyone these days know what a salon is? People still have a vague idea in France, the last country where conversation has preserved a certain glamour. The salon is a social institution no more. To enter a salon in 1830 was as important an affair as entering the office of a high government official is today. Why, when I was twenty, wasn't I given Stendhalian recipes for life in 1940? They would have cut short my gropings and miseries by several years.

This recipe for entering a salon is a splendid example of a

recipe for desperate cases, which are those situations one lands in when one doesn't know what to do. Any attitude is better than no attitude at all. To preserve the expression one had as one climbed the stairs is just as effective as the naïve smile, the vacuous and foolish expression, the look of admiration or respect, or even the arrogance which the inexperienced assume before an imposing group of people.

Those who talk little easily acquire a reputation for profundity or even wit. A man who disembarks with the grave and absorbed air which is inevitably produced by the ascent of twenty-three steps passes without difficulty for a man of self-respect and anything but a simpleton. To leave one's attitude to chance, when one has no alternative, is also the maxim of a hero, who makes use of whatever is to hand, or a courageous soldier who takes advantage of the accidents of the terrain. Nothing is more fatal than to be caught unawares. Any rampart, even one run up at the last minute, is preferable to open ground.

27 *Here is his recipe for one's first duel: "While your adversary is taking aim at you, look at a tree and concentrate on counting its leaves. One preoccupation distracts from another, graver preoccupation. While aiming at your adversary, recite two lines of Latin verse; this will prevent you from firing too hastily and offset the five per cent of emotion which has sent so many bullets twenty feet higher than they should have gone."*

STENDHAL fought his first duel in 1797, at the age of fourteen and a half, with his schoolmate Odru. He describes this duel with great pleasure and pride in *La Vie de Henry Brulard*. It took place outside the ramparts of Grenoble. Odru was a giant; he was a foot taller than Beyle and threatened to thrash him as a substitute for shooting him. It was he who fired first. While he did so, Henri gazed fixedly at a piece of rock above him, shaped like a trapezium, the same piece that could be seen from his Aunt Élisabeth's window beside the roof of the Church of St. Louis.

The "second," prudent like all children, hadn't loaded the pistols. But Beyle was unaware of this. He believed he was really facing death and heroically stared at his rock while thinking of something else. At fifty, this profoundly modest man, who was always ready to denigrate himself, wrote of this behavior: "I wasn't pretending; I was completely natural, not showing off, but very brave." "In moments of great danger," he wrote again, "I am natural and simple." This resembles Julien Sorel, who went to the guillotine "simply, decorously and without any affectation. . . ." Here is a case of supreme good form. Beyle, going home along the Rue Très-Cloîtres with his "second," Maurice Diday, confided to the latter how, to avoid being afraid, he had stared at the piece of rock above Seyssins. "You must never repeat that," replied Diday. "Such an admission must never cross your lips!" And he scolded him severely. "I was quite astonished," writes Stendhal, "and, on thinking it over, deeply shocked by this rebuke." Such a reaction does honor to its author. There are few boys of fourteen of sufficiently formed character to stand up for their private feelings against prejudice. Here, prejudice in favor of superhuman courage and dauntlessness—both obviously most unlikely. At fourteen and a half, Beyle already had a passionate love of truth. Not to admit that he had been *a little* frightened during his duel would have seemed to him intolerable hypocrisy, and stupid.

On the other hand, this little hero felt a dreadful remorse for having allowed this business with Odru to be rigged. How could he dare admire the Cid after not having really fought? The whole passage in *Brulard* about the duel with Odru is wonderful. It is a rare piece of child psychology and has the complete ring of truth, but of a noble truth. For truth can also be noble. It is not solely the attribute of base souls, *à la* Sainte-Beuve, or microscopic ones *à la* Jules Renard.*

Thirty years separate the duel with Odru from the recipe reported by Mérimée. For Stendhal these thirty years had been filled with excitement, ideas, adventures, lies and, above all, a wide experience of artistic creation. All great artists,

---

* "Base souls above all depict base feelings, even though they condemn them." (Aristotle, *Poetry*, IV, 7.) At certain epochs, people do not even trouble to condemn them.

that is to say those who have an inexorable love of truth and lay it bare at a glance, are liars. They lie quite simply, just as they automatically give their works those finishing touches which make everything a little larger than life and "put it across." They lie just as, in a novel, they transpose. They lie, finally, because they know that artistic truth is the product of many distortions, reconstructions and disguises.

The finest pictures in our galleries are lies, and Michelangelo is just as much a liar as Giotto, Cézanne or Ingres. Stendhal lies in a similar fashion. He is right to translate pink into green, and black into pink. But is it still a lie? I would rather say that it is carrying truth to its extreme limits. The eye of a great painter, like the heart of a great writer, perceives rays invisible to ordinary eyes.

When Stendhal gave Mérimée his recipe for a duel, he was thinking of Odru, of course, and of his other duels; he was thinking of his great moments of simple courage (no showing off) and of his little fears, but he never mentioned these. He provided his recipe unadorned, like a moralist, like Rivarol, Chamfort or Joubert, who compresses his experience in tablet form. That is lying, in this subtle sense. To play the moralist, even laughingly, is to imply a wide experience and sustained thought. In fact, Stendhal does not quote his sources. He knew that one creates a deeper impression that way.

I am familiar with the way in which the minds of men of letters work. They get besotted about their ideas, as if they were mistresses, and use them for self-advertisement in society. These showy liaisons last from a fortnight to three months. One is astonished to find in their books what they have casually remarked to one the evening before. It wouldn't surprise me if Stendhal had confided his recipe for a duel to Mérimée at about the time when he was writing *Brulard*, while still full of the pleasure he had from remembering his duel with Odru, forgotten for thirty-five years, and the joy of recording it. To offer as the fruit of experience at fifty something one discovered by chance at fourteen by obeying the right instinct—this is one of those gratifying little bits of semi-insincerity in which artists constantly indulge.

28

"If you find yourself alone with a woman, I give you five minutes to prepare yourself for the prodigious effort of saying to her, 'I love you.' Tell yourself, 'I am a coward if I haven't said this within five minutes.' It doesn't matter in what way or in what terms you pay your compliment. Enough that the ice should be broken and you should be fully determined to despise yourself if your courage fails you."

Just as one can read in *Brulard* the story of the duel with Odru, whence comes the preceding recipe, so can this one be found in *Le Rouge et le Noir*, with Julien taking his mistress' hand under pain of death. This scene, played in the dark under "the vast lime tree a few yards from the house," is so true, so charged with emotion that I sometimes think I haven't read it but lived it. I would add the following consideration: that a serious writer (as Stendhal was) never knows how to trace the dividing line between his work and his life. Each nourishes the other reciprocally. The fact is that a great work is always a reflection of nature. It copies nature, but nature for her part makes use of it too. The recipe of Julien Sorel, a character in a novel, benefits real people equally well.

It is not my intention here to discuss "Stendhal and women," which must have been done twenty times under one title or another; my only aim is to rove through the soul of this wonderful man, to admire the landscape and sometimes point out some detail. As far as the present recipe is concerned, I refer the reader back to Chapter 7. This is typical of Beyle's attitude to life and illustrates the contradiction of Don Juan versus the man of sensibility. It is imperative to say "I love you" to a pretty woman whom one does not otherwise desire, since it is difficult, since it is a conquest of oneself. Directly the idea of such a declaration has crossed one's mind, the obligation to make it asserts itself on pain of contempt. Stendhal went into love as Turenne went into battle, trembling but with unshakable courage. Stendhal's soul was as full of love as Turenne's was full of war. The fear makes no difference at all. On the contrary, it perhaps makes the joys of love or war even keener.

Plainly, Stendhal's recipe is valid only for very young, inexperienced men, who let chances of happiness slip by due to timidity or blindness. After twenty-six or -seven, it is worthless or merely leads to rebuffs. After that age, in fact, a man with some knowledge of love and an impartial desire for all pretty women grasps the imponderables, understands the most imperceptible advances and shows infallible daring. But, following the example of all Stendhal's maxims or recipes, this one recommends the most difficult course and does so in the grand manner. Its efficacity derives from the fact that it makes the optional unavoidable, translates into an act what was only a moment before a stray impulse.

To give recipes is the height of honesty. It means that one is sure of one's ideas and very earnest, that one isn't afraid to pass from speculation to practice, and that one truly wishes one's fellows well. This never fails to provoke mockery. They call one a cook. Most people get drunk on theories, as if they were poems. Prudent persons know that life is a difficult business and that recipes are precious guides to one's conduct in it.

I would like to note here a recipe I concocted for myself in 1943, which in its matter-of-factness has something Stendhalian about it and of which I must confess I was therefore extremely proud. I had been arrested by the militia, which ably copied the methods of the Gestapo and inflicted rather savage brutalities on its prisoners. In my cell, waiting to be interrogated, I wondered what I should do to avoid talking (that is to say, betraying the names of my comrades, the whereabouts of our stores of arms or our clandestine printing presses, and so on) if they put out my eyes or cut off my ears. Well, I thought, I must just act as if the thing were inevitable, as if it weren't a question of brutalities inflicted by the hands of men but of maladies inflicted by nature. No "revelation" stops the agonies of a renal colic or a mastoid. I drew up a scale, comparing the tortures I anticipated to the different afflictions to which one is exposed during sixty or eighty years of life. For instance, a thumbscrew seemed to me the equivalent of a boil. I thought of the soldiers of yore, who had arms or legs amputated on the battlefield without any anesthetic. I calculated I could hold out up to cirrhosis of the liver and cancer of the prostate. After that . . . Hell, we should see. I was lucky enough to escape fairly soon, which saved me from having to put my recipe to the test. Even so, I think it was a good one, and it greatly fortified my courage in that delicate situation. It might, I think, still prove useful to someone, for the world has reverted to extreme barbarity and men have again begun to apply torture as vile as in the heyday of the Inquisition.

29

Beyle, who preached "love-taste," was very capable of "love-passion." There was one lady whose name he could never mention without a catch in his voice. In 1836 I saw him again after a long absence. We had arranged to meet about thirty leagues outside Paris and had a thousand things to tell each other. We talked at great length that evening, walking up and down the public promenade of a little town, which is to say in one of the loneliest places in France. There he told me of his love affairs with deep emotion. It is the only time I ever saw him weep. An affection of many years' standing was no longer returned. His mistress was becoming sensible and he had remained as wild as he was when he was twenty. "How can you still love me?" she asked. "I am forty-five." "For me," Beyle told me, "she is the same age she was when she gave herself to me for the first time." He foresaw the disruption in the near future of a liaison he had always cherished. One thought to which he referred everything was about to be obliterated. He described to me the past recklessness of this woman, today so prudent, and his memories carried him away. Then, with the powers of observation which never deserted him, he detailed all the little symptoms, all the signs of increasing indifference which he had remarked. Lo-gic was not forgotten. "After all," he said, "her behavior is reasonable. She used to love whist, she loves it no longer; so much the worse for me if I still love whist. She comes from a country where ridicule is the worst of misfortunes. To love at her age is ridiculous. Eighteen months ago she risked this misfortune for me. For me

it is eighteen months of happiness that I have stolen." We
argued at length over the truth of these lines from Dante:

> . . . Nessum maggior dolore
> Che ricordasi del tempo felice
> Nella miseria.

He maintained that Dante was wrong, and that the memories
of past happiness remain happiness everywhere and always.
I remember how I defended the poet. Today it seems to me
that Beyle was right.

THE LITTLE TOWN in question was Laon, and the lady whose
name Beyle couldn't mention without a catch in his voice was
Mme. la Comtesse Clémentine Curial. Nothing is as painful as
a mistress who "becomes sensible." Mérimée's little phrase,
without seeming to, says exactly what is needed: "One thought
to which he referred everything was about to be obliterated."
Such, in effect, is the nature of the unhappiness caused when a
lover leaves one; he who is deserted suddenly loses what
formed the esential element of his life: the being whom he
associated, not with his every thought, perhaps, but with all
his movements and all his actions, and over whose feelings he
worried before his own. To have to be concerned solely with
oneself after having been solely concerned with another is to
fall back into nothingness. But these considerations are banality itself. Everyone knows what it is to be crossed in love;
everyone knows the desert into which a man is cast who loves
but is suddenly no longer beloved. He is torn in two, one half
of his life has interred the other half. Stendhal's sorrows are as
beautiful as Mozart's operas, for, unlike most people, who kill
their grief by starving it, he nourished them with his full
imagination, which intermittently raised up his past joys before him so lavishly that he couldn't deprive himself of this

kind of happiness. Solitude favors these agonizing but sweet visions.

A little biography has to be interposed, however—that is to say, conjecture and fiction. Beyle became the lover of Mme. Curial, known as "Menti," in 1824. She broke with him in 1826—that is, ten years before the meeting at Laon. In the meantime Stendhal had at least one passion, Giulia Rinieri. But time doesn't seem to count for men of sensibility who preserve the memory of their emotions. Once the heart becomes vacant, old emotions come violently flooding in again. The image of past joys revives in brilliant hues which are those of life itself. I remember how, when I was young, I sometimes used to flee in the middle of some pleasure or happiness; I didn't hesitate to cut it short, so that I might quietly savor its details in solitude. In other words, the memory of the event gave me greater pleasure than the event itself, which passed all too quickly, catching me up in a whirlwind in which I lost all control. This, certainly, was a characteristic of an imaginative man or an artist. I was like a painter incapable of working on the spot, who notes down landscapes in a sketchbook and then paints the picture at leisure in his studio.

I detect something analogous in Stendhal, always traveling, always solitary, always noting down his feelings and analyzing them (that is, enriching them) in the silence of his study. How his heart transformed his two years of passion for Menti into ten is obviously something I wouldn't dare try to explain, but I can guess at it. To be left, even if one has longed one-self a hundred times over to leave, causes a scar which never heals. To be left means that your love has not died of exhaustion or old age but has been murdered, killed in its prime. *Chagrin d'amour* leaves delightful memories. When its keen edge is blunted, a general impression of happiness remains, which is always very sweet to recall. The heart feels as it were ennobled. The memories of artists are works of art, considerably retouched. "And Menti, how can I describe the grief into which she plunged me when she left me?" writes Stendhal in *Brulard*. Such a phrase has nothing to do with literature; it is impossible to cast any doubts on it. It is a sincere question, such as any ordinary man might write to a trusted friend. But it is also beyond doubt that this kind of grief forms part and parcel with the joys that preceded it, that it is indivisible from them and that its memory is a *happy* memory.

A woman who has left you, after having loved you and proved it by recklessness, leaves a dazzling trail in the heart. A woman one has left is not the same thing, even though she loved you far more, even though she was a thousand times more reckless. It is the love one feels which counts; the love one inspires has value only through that. Should your love die before the love you inspire, the latter loses much of its color and charm. Of course, like all love, it recaptures these in memory; but am I wrong when I say that a love tragically disrupted leaves a deeper scar than a love ended in boredom? Yes, I am probably wrong, for I am generalizing. The women one has made unhappy also fill one's heart with delightful ghosts. One's remorse for having made them suffer has charms as great as one's regret for having suffered.

"Clémentine is the one who caused me the greatest pain when she left me. But is this pain comparable to the one inflicted by Métilde, who did not want to tell me she loved me?" writes Stendhal, again in *Brulard*. This Métilde Dembowski, whom Stendhal loved passionately, to the point of seriously thinking of blowing his brains out, and who gave him nothing in return, was an extraordinary object of "crystallization."* It

---

* From Stendhal's third preface to *De l'Amour:* "The public had to be brought to accept the new word "crystallization," propounded as the vivid expression of that collection of strange hallucinations which one fancies to be true and even beyond dispute with regard to the woman one loves."

seems that Beyle traveled the whole road of love alone and almost without encouragement. He never ceased, in his private writings, to adore her, admire her, and cover her with flowers. All the same, one can't help feeling a keen dislike for her. She had a great soul, says Stendhal, a noble character in the Spanish style, such as he doted on; but she was also terribly afraid of what her neighbors would think, and this trait appalls me. It doesn't go with the "great soul." A soul afflicted with *espagnolisme* doesn't reduce a Stendhal to despair. This despair rather puzzles me. I find it hard to see how a woman who has never been one's mistress, who has never added to intimacy of spirit the vital one of the body, can lead one to those desolate regions, that "desert East" in which Beyle languished for over three years. The fact remains, however. This can only mean that I am not made the same way as he was.

What is to follow now will surely incur the scorn of the professional Stendhalians, who will refer me to twenty scholarly works which I haven't read and never will. The account of the meeting at Laon doesn't tally with what I know of my hero. M. Martineau, in fact, says that Beyle did not leave Civitavecchia, where he had spent two and a half years and where he was slightly taken up with loving the Contessa Cini, until May 11, 1836. In Paris, M. Martineau goes on, "he wanted to find a heart to love. Giulia Rinieri-Martini, who had returned to Paris since her marriage, proved reticent. Clémentine Curial didn't want to stir up dead ashes. In vain he asked another woman to marry him."

To invite Menti ten years later to renew a liaison with him was typical of Stendhal. He must have cherished this project for a long time, adorning it with all his memories. Perhaps Menti felt herself yielding—he was so persuasive! Even so, this doesn't explain the "eighteen months of stolen happiness." I think that here Beyle was lying. But what matter? It seems to me quite natural that he should arrange a meeting with his best friend, the Comte Gazul, in the department of the Aisne, to tell him a piece of fiction. After all, the lie related only to the *facts*, not at all to the feelings, and if Beyle wept it was because he was genuinely unhappy. When people given to secrecy feel a need to unburden their souls, they travesty the causes, which are the events, but speak the truth as regards the effects, which are their sorrows or joys, that is to say the essentials. Beyle felt a need to talk to someone of Mérimée's genius, who would understand the "little symptoms" and "signs of indifference" and appreciate the way in which they were observed. He also needed to talk of the love of whist and the absurdity of loving at forty-five to someone who understood this language. Moreover, the correct assessment of the situation, the sense of responsibility ("so much the worse for me if I still love whist"), the idea of effecting a cure through art (clinical examination of the extinction of a passion), the small margin of profit ("eighteen months of stolen happiness") make this anecdote, whether false or true, an exemplary story whose moral is extremely healthy and strong. I find even his philosophy delightful; to say (and feel) that "memories of past happiness remain happiness everywhere and always" is truly making the best of things.

30

He had had another love affair in Italy of which he avoided any mention. However, he himself described to me the tragic end of this love. The lady had a very jealous husband, or so she maintained, and this obliged her to take great precautions. Meetings could only be rare and wrapped in the deepest mystery. To avoid any suspicion, Beyle resigned himself to hiding in a little town about ten leagues distant from the fair one's dwelling. When he received an assignation, he set off incognito and changed coaches several times in order to baffle the spies he believed to surround him; finally, arriving after dark, well muffled in a stone-gray cloak, he was admitted to his mistress' house by a chambermaid of proven discretion. Everything went well for a time, until this chambermaid, who had either quarreled with her mistress or been won over by Beyle's generosity, made a staggering revelation: Monsieur was not jealous, and Madame, despite the good faith of Italian ladies, which he constantly upheld in contrast to the coquetry of our own, insisted on all this mystery only to prevent Beyle from meeting his rival or, to tell the truth, rivals, for there were several, and this the chambermaid offered to prove to him. Beyle accepted. He came to the town one day when he was not expected and, hidden by the maid in a dark little closet, he saw himself with his very own eyes, *through a hole arranged in the partition, being betrayed a few feet from his hiding place.*

"You might perhaps think," added Beyle, "that I rushed out of the closet to stab them? Not at all. I felt I was watching the most comic scene, and my sole concern was to prevent myself

from bursting out laughing, lest I should spoil the mystery. I left my dark closet as discreetly as I had entered it, thinking only of the absurdity of the adventure and laughing to myself —even so, full of contempt for the lady and, all in all, well content to have regained my freedom. I went to have an ice and met some people I knew who were most struck by my air of gaiety combined with a certain distraction. They told me I looked like a man who had just been lucky in love. While I talked with them and ate my ice, I was frequently shaken by irrepressible laughter and the puppets I had watched an hour before kept dancing before my eyes. Back at my lodgings, I slept as usual.

"The next morning, the vision of the dark closet had ceased to seem merely comic. I felt it to be ugly, sad and dirty. Each day this image became more depressing and repellent, each day added a further weight to my unhappiness. For eighteen months I remained as if stupefied, incapable of any work, unfit to write, talk or think. I felt oppressed by an intolerable pain, without being able clearly to account to myself for what I was feeling. There is no greater misfortune, for it saps all one's energy. After that, somewhat recovered from this overwhelming lethargy, I felt a strange curiosity to discover all the infidelities done to me. This had a terrible effect on me; and yet I felt a kind of physical pleasure in picturing her to myself in the course of her numerous betrayals.

"I took my revenge, but stupidly, in flippancy. She was deeply upset over our rupture and begged my forgiveness with tears. A ridiculous pride made me repulse her with scorn. I seem to see her still, following me, clinging to my coat and dragging herself on her knees down a long gallery. I was a fool not to forgive her, for assuredly she never loved me as much as she did that day."

137

THE READER is requested to turn back to the first page of this book and reread the title of one of the versions of Mérimée's little work which I have taken for my text: *H.B. par un des Quarante.* This was written by an Academician of 1850. It was a sort of obituary notice for a man who had existed, whom they had known, who was a noted writer and even, from time to time, an official figure. How amazing to find it including this story, worthy of Faublas or Casanova's *Memoirs*, this scabrous and moving comedy, this brutal *École des Femmes?* Today we get nothing but heavy pornography without morality, or official panegyrics, and the literary world is roughly divided into two categories of writer: the smutty and the asinine. There is no mistaking the spirit in which Mérimée describes Beyle's amorous mishap; it reflects the emotion that dominated his life—a simple love of truth. Mérimée was neither a purveyor of smut nor an ass, but a man for whom the truth posed no problems. It is always *a good thing to tell,* under any circumstances. Besides, Beyle, who was cast in the same mold as his friend, would have been the last person to be shocked to find this indiscreet and deplorable story in his obituary notice. He himself told much worse ones in his private writings. He never made the foolish mistake of being ashamed of what *really* happened and never sought to suppress a story by silence. There is something indescribably alive, one might even say eternal, about what he saw "with his very own eyes," and this Mérimée grasped and felt himself when he subsequently recorded it.

One can share the feeling with which Stendhal told Mérimée this story. They were both lovers of bizarre and romantic situations. Next, Beyle played a part in it which, far from being impressive, was that of a simpleton tricked by a slut (a hussy). Lastly, this provided material for many highly diverting discussions and comments.

The hussy was Signora Angela Pietragrua, "a sublime whore in the Italian manner, à la Lucretia Borgia," whose name Mérimée knew. Men find it amusing to describe their love affairs to each other, I mean to their friends. But it is only the happy affairs which they are usually so willing to describe, in order to enhance their reputations and fill the others with envy and admiration. It is to the glory of Stendhal's soul that the only two love affairs of which he spoke to his friend were either tragic or burlesque. This was because, with his good taste, he held these two alone to be worthy of interest on account of their strangeness.

The analysis of Beyle's feelings, excellently summarized by Mérimée, illustrates this passage from *Brulard:* "I have never been attentive to women—not enough; I was only ever taken up with the woman I loved, and when I wasn't in love I dreamed of the spectacle of humanity or delighted in reading Montesquieu or Walter Scott." In effect, Beyle, in Milan, watching the goings-on of the shameless Angela from his dark closet, didn't feel at all like the Cardinal de Bernis, whom Casanova shows us in a similar situation in Venice and enchanted to find himself there. An infinite distance separates Stendhal from the libertines. He was resolutely antilibertine. The proof lies in the fact that the spectacle of licentiousness made him laugh. The gravity of the libertine's gestures, as he solemnly acts a part to himself and achieves his pleasure through more or less feigned attitudes, seemed to him an offense against nature and truth and hence irresistibly comic. Even more than feeling, it seems to me, libertines must kill all sense of the ridiculous in themselves, in order to attain that superior indifference which makes them perform the most puerile acts for their physical delight.

Stendhal, always at war against the ridiculous, like a good Frenchman, feared it and sensed it with the speed of lightning. In the dark closet, the absurdity of his position and what he saw completely absorbed him. One has the impression that four or five emotions swept simultaneously through his heart —horror, disgust, jealousy and anger—but were immediately brushed aside by his critical mind as being unsuited to the situation. This was *comic*, in the best spirit of light novels and bedroom farces; objectively it formed a perfect collection of absurdities. Lo-gic therefore ordained that one should burst out laughing. In a very subtle and clever man, used to ruling himself with an iron hand, logic affects the heart at the same time as the mind.

". . . full of contempt for the lady and, all in all, well content to have regained my freedom." Here are two reactions accurately pinned down. But how hard it is, a hundred and forty-two years later, to follow a love affair through all its circumvolutions and lies! I don't think Beyle ever had much respect for Signora Pietragrua, a woman of marvelous beauty, apparently, but compliant and dissolute; he loved her by and large out of pique (because she had resisted him, thirteen years before, when he was a young dragoon) and carnal suitability. It is a pretty triumph when one is thirty-one to have the unapproachable goddess of one's teens. Anyway, perfect beauty always attracts a lover; the joy, the intoxicating vanity it gives him to know that he is the sole possessor of this treasure makes life gay, induces a gay happiness. This and love are as like as two peas; and how is one to distinguish true love from what resembles it?

When they have exhausted the charms of a new love, people afflicted with a spirit of contradiction always involuntarily think of all the things that love has caused them to miss: other loves, or work, or solitude. Even if they have loved their mistress to distraction, they become aware that she has torn them from themselves, and they bear her a slight grudge for it. For Stendhal, after having witnessed the frightful spectacle of his misfortune, to cry to himself, "Long live freedom!" was the impulse of an artist, of a hard-working man who was perhaps a little weary of wasting his time hiding ten leagues outside Milan, changing coaches and going about in a stone-colored cloak. At the end of a week, romance becomes routine and one is conscious only of its extreme complications.

To switch in a flash from love to contempt is not without charm. One tells oneself that contempt kills love or at least "decrystallizes" it; this is an illusion, but it provides a good reason for ridding oneself of a love. At any rate, contempt prescribes action, it makes ruptures easy and legitimate, it allays the conscience; it even engenders a kind of bitter gaiety, as witness Beyle's gusts of laughter at the café while eating his ice. He was torn between the comedy of the situation and the tragedy of his feelings. Still contemptuous, he opted for the comedy. By the next morning, contempt had died away. After the excitement caused by so much absurdity, his heart recovered its balance and vexation settled into its appointed place. The adventure appeared in its true light, which was ugly, sad and dirty, at least in its victim's eyes. It can happen that a man full of purity and honor finds himself dragged by imprudence or thoughtlessness into some dishonorable business. He suddenly opens his eyes, he awakens, he sees his destiny bound up with that of a set of crooks, he has embarked on a vessel he never even imagined he had boarded. He feels an outcast, soiled, dragged down, transported into a sulphurous world where he is condemned to live from now on. This is a terrible disaster. A soul goes into exile.

The day following the episode of the dark closet, Beyle's soul went into an exile which lasted a year and a half. This bright spirit spent a year and a half in a land of darkness. If you prefer another comparison, Beyle, in his dark closet, contracted a malady of the soul, a leprosy, a wasting decline which he was able to cure only by cauterizing, by causing himself "intolerable pain." His air of gaiety at the café "combined with a certain distraction" is poignant. These are the moments of aberration of a man haunted by an idea that is laying him waste.

What I find hard to understand about this story is that Beyle should have accepted the good offices of the chambermaid. Why didn't he refuse to listen to the little tramp? Or why, having listened to her, didn't he ask Angela straight out if it was true that he was a dupe and a cuckold? To agree to let oneself be shut up in a dark closet is to be avid indeed for sensations and presuming greatly on one's strength of spirit. It is already contempt.

On the other hand, one couldn't find any fault with the conclusion Stendhal draws from the drama: "I took my revenge, but stupidly, in flippancy," and so on. This reveals a man sure of his heart, who judges things only in relation to himself. Ninety-nine men out of a hundred would be sincerely scandalized by this morality, which is high, just and totally sentimental. It is by feeling thus, and not fearing to admit it, that one takes the shortest cut to happiness. Prejudices, self-esteem and fear of public opinion force most people to make infinite detours. Time, alas, passes swiftly. Death snatches them up halfway there.

31

Beyle's constant preoccupation was the study of the passions. When some provincial asked him what was his profession, he would gravely reply, "Observer of the human heart." (One day he said this to a fool who nearly fell over backward, imagining that it was a euphemism for a police spy.) Of every story which could serve to shed light on some corner of the heart, he always singled out what he called the feature, *that is to say the word or action which revealed the passion. Dragging herself on her knees—that for him was the feature of the little story I have just told and, following his habit of drawing general conclusions from facts particular to himself, he held that this manner of behavior was the pure expression of remorse and passionate love.*

I⊤ HAS suddenly occurred to me while reading this paragraph of Mérimée's that the two authors who maintain that Stendhal was a police spy have perhaps made the same mistake as the fool who nearly fell over backward. I hope this is so. Stendhal, from wherever he is, must have guffawed as he read them. To fool people still, a hundred and fifteen years after one's death, is not given to everybody!

Stendhal's sally, "An observer of the human heart," seems very moving today. What he proffered with such comic gravity, making fun of provincials, himself and society, was a future truth. His posts in the civil service were successively assistant to the war commissioners, auditor to the Privy Coun-

cil, surveyor of the imperial household and French consul at
Civitavecchia; in 1814 he nearly became prefect of Le Mans.
But his true profession was in fact the one he stated. It is as
such that he has gone down to posterity. There is always an
element of seriousness, of that profound and rather sad, because true, seriousness in the jokes of great men. They make
them sparkle with humor, but one could take them literally
without being wrong. The light, gratuitous wit which induces
carefree laughter amuses by its fantasy and above all means
nothing because it isn't based on sincere observation; this language coined for social occasions is not their concern.

Love of the "feature" proves a dual vocation, as a mathematician and a caricaturist. The "feature" is the postulate of a
character or a passion. As for the caricature, consisting of
exaggerating one particular aspect which symbolizes, sums up
and typifies the whole, this is the exact procedure of the artistic
mind, which simplifies and synthesizes almost by instinct.
Great artists (even the gentlest, such as Vinci, Mozart and
Puvis de Chavannes) have had the gift of caricature, which
implies an eagle eye for the little revealing distortion whereby
the soul expresses itself.

When Beyle was seven, a friend of his grandfather's, M. Bar-
thélemy d'Orbane, a famous Grenoble lawyer, taught him to
make faces. This was an art at which he made rapid progress
and which he still practiced at the age of fifty-three. In the
Privy Council, in the presence of Napoleon, he would amuse
himself dangerously by mimicking the self-important air of
the terrible Comte Régnault de Saint-Jean-d'Angély sitting
twelve feet away from him, "particularly when, the better to
hear the choleric Abbé Louis seated on the other side of the
room, he pulled down the inordinately long collars of his
shirt." Stendhal adds, "This instinct, or this art, which I owe
to M. d'Orbane, has made me many enemies. Even today the
sober Fiori reproaches me for the concealed, or rather ill-

concealed, irony in the right corner of my mouth." The word "instinct" is very important. For myself, I draw the following conclusion: that the childish pranks of great men, like their jokes, have a serious basis. Stendhal, with his faces and imitations, still remained an "observer of the human heart." He made his caricatures with his face. In aping the Comte Régnault pulling down the points of his collar to listen, he was penetrating a little into this man's character. When he gave his imitations in society, the laughter they caused signified "How right that is! How *well observed!*" I have noticed that people who are not responsive to caricatures, who don't grasp their truth, understand nothing about art as a whole.

The habit of drawing general conclusions from facts particular to himself, which Mérimée gives as one of Stendhal's attributes, is an excellent plan for a writer. To know oneself is to know the world. Man is the rule of three of the universe. The writer has to regard himself as a microcosm. It is by this means that one can describe Mosca without ever having been a minister; this is how a citizen under "King Philippe" can accurately catch the way men talked during the Renaissance.

 *To wind up the subject of love: Beyle believed that happiness was possible in this world only for a man in love. "Everything takes on a beautiful color for him," he used to say. "I should like to be in love with Mademoiselle Flore of the Variétés, and then I wouldn't envy Don Juan himself."*

I AM FULLY AWARE that in writing this book I should constantly refer the reader to the relevant passages in the relevant works by Stendhal. At least, any serious commentator would do so. I should like to say, however, that at one time or another in my life I have read the whole of Stendhal, including his *Journal*, his letters and the smallest scraps of his ideas jotted down on odd bits of paper in a Franco-Anglo-Italian telegraphese. On the other hand, I have read almost nothing about Stendhal; almost the only things I know are Alain's admirable comments, as good as Stendhal himself, and the article in which Sainte-Beuve tells him some "home truths," for which read truths about Sainte-Beuve.

I might add that, at the cost of a certain amount of tedious labor, I could quite easily append to Mérimée's paragraphs all the corresponding references in Stendhal's works. This task seems to me worse than futile. I write for his admirers. I write for *the happy few* who, like myself, are mad about Stendhal, who feel that special, unique love that no other writer has ever managed to inspire.* These readers need no references. Or, rather, everything for them is a reference; they don't need me to indicate them, for they know their Stendhal as well as they know themselves; they have read him in such a way that their hearts secrete a little music similar to his own.

Mérimée's paragraph which heads this chapter has for a paraphrase the whole book called *De l'Amour*. I have reread this masterpiece, just to play the pedant for once, and I have been rewarded for it. Each line is as overwhelming and thrilling as in a good novel. Stendhal wrote *De l'Amour* at the height of his despair induced by the harshness of Métilde. It is the opposite of a cold and didactic essay; behind the arguments, the disguises, the examples, the apothegms, the anecdotes, the classifications, one follows hard on the heels of Beyle's soul. But this is still not the whole truth; *De l'Amour* is better than a novel, it is the behind-the-scenes, the wings of a novel, in which one finds all the things that, in the novel itself, disappear but in fact constitute its subterranean riches. It is a coffer stuffed with diamonds. All the diamonds of love are there, not made up into jewelry, as a jeweler's creations, but in raw bulk. Love is depicted in its entirety. I can't understand the sort of obscurity from which *De l'Amour* suffers among Stendhal's works. There are few essays in which one can read: "I always tremble for fear that I have written only a sigh when I think I have noted a truth." One can write the memoirs of one's heart in the form of a treatise. Here is the proof.

For a complete understanding of Mérimée's five lines, I refer the reader more particularly to the following chapters in *De l'Amour:* II, XI, XVII, XXXII, XXXIII, XXXV and XXXIX-C of Book One, together with Maxims 11 and 42 of the *Fragments*

---

* "With Stendhal, the man is so special that there are no half measures; one either adores him or detests him." (Paul Léautaud, *The Stendhal Club*, 1905.)

divers. I also draw attention to Chapter LIX of Book Two, in which the author compares Don Juan and Werther. This contains a description of Don Juan's character which, in a few pages, far excels what so many contemporary authors have said in as many volumes on this character. There is also a judgment and condemnation of Don Juan which seem to me the essence of good sense: the author demonstrates that Don Juan had less happiness than Werther or Saint-Preux. The wonderful thing is that virtue never comes into it; or, if Stendhal mentions the word, it is not in the currently accepted sense.

"Don Juan's happiness," he says, "is merely vanity based, it is true, on circumstances brought about by much wit and activity; but he must feel that the humblest general who wins a battle, the humblest prefect who keeps control of a province, enjoys a more remarkable delight than his own, whereas the joy of the Duc de Nemours when Mme. de Clèves tells him she loves him is, I think, greater than Napoleon's joy at Marengo."

He adds, "The curse of inconstancy is boredom; the curse of love-passion is despair and death. People take heed of the despairs of love; they provide material for gossip; nobody pays any attention to blasé old rakes who are dying of boredom and with whom Paris is paved." Another remark in Werther's favor: "The man who trembles is never bored. The pleasures of love are always in proportion to his fear."

Here is another amusing saying, which I can't resist in passing, for the sake of the hotheads who have discovered the Marquis de Sade and made him into a sort of saint: When one has the misfortune not to love anyone but feels like a little distraction, Stendhal advises one to practice "love-taste, without horrors. The horrors always come from a small soul which needs to reassure itself as to its own merits." The libertines I have met and to whom I would impart a little philosophy, if not profundity, have astonished me by their bigoted and maniacal character. They have the same niggling souls, I think, as the collectors of stamps or clocks, the professional punsters and the matchbox fans.

To return to Mlle. Flore of the Variétés, I presume that Beyle wanted to love like Werther and not like Don Juan. And why not Mlle. Flore, if she is pleasing and affectionate, and if she is modest? Let us suffer for Mlle. Flore. The Don Juans may laugh, but we shall never be bored, which is the main thing.

33

Next to love, literature occupied the largest place in Beyle's affections. He loved reading and wrote incessantly. Nulla dies sine linea, *he often said to me, reproaching me for my laziness. Whatever signs of negligence one may find in his books, they were nonetheless worked over at great length. All his books were copied out several times before being delivered to the printer; but his corrections were hardly ever concerned with style. He always wrote rapidly, changing his thoughts but troubling little over form. He even expressed contempt for style and maintained that an author had achieved perfection when men remembered his ideas without being able to recall how they were worded. Full of hatred for affectation and pretentiousness, he was merciless to writers who strive to combine words that are startling when juxtaposed, to polish their sentences and to give the most trivial thoughts a bizarre twist for the sake of effect. Our great prose writers of the seventeenth and eighteenth centuries were for him the object of sincere and heartfelt admiration. He reread them ceaselessly, in order to preserve himself, so he said, from the contagion of the fashionable style of his day.*

ART AND LOVE are clearly the two essentials of life. Politics seem to me a fairly good substitute for art; had I not had a vocation as a writer, I would gladly have made a career as a politician. True, democracy has taken much of the charm out of politics as an art. To become a statesman today one must begin by deafening the public with speeches or being a town councilor and waste ten years of one's life spouting banalities to the great unwashed. Failing which, even if one were inspired by the most disinterested concern for the public weal, one is treated as a fascist.

Beyle had bouts of political ambition under the Empire, but he never behaved like a truly ambitious man. At the height of his success, he continued to keep his journal, to which he confided things that would have struck his contemporaries as quite preposterous and that appear to us sublime. The fact, for instance, that what he liked above all in Milan was a certain smell of ordure in the streets. He also continued to have love affairs *à la* Werther, which was most unbecoming a potential minister. On March 5, 1815, he learned of Napoleon's return to France, but, "mad for love of Gina Gr——," meaning Angela Pietragrua, he stayed in Milan. This choice is categorical. To Napoleon he preferred the beautiful Angela, whom he was to see from his dark closet ten months later conscientiously making a fool of him.

To put art and love uppermost among his preoccupations, to devote the best part of his time to them, is typical of a man without vanity, who takes the shortest cuts to happiness. It seems to me that if one takes the precaution of allowing for a little idleness, a little free and lonely boredom between love and literature, one procures a full and perfect life.

"Next to love, literature occupied the largest place . . ." says Mérimée. Yes, love is more *diverting* than literature, it provides more romantic and violent pleasures. Literature comes after. Besides, with Stendhal it was entirely nurtured by love. Chronologically, sensation precedes observation. But I don't think that Mérimée was concerned with chronology. He was speaking of taste. What could be more normal than to put love uppermost in one's affections? Nature inclines us that way. Even so, with most men nature soon fades into the background. At twenty-five or thirty, one begins to despise love in favor of a career, or marriage, or the races, or business; as soon as the first powerful demands of one's body are appeased, one is caught up by vanity and contents oneself with passing affairs, which are swift and inconsequential caricatures of love. I have noticed that most people run away from love as if it were the plague. They are frightened of it; love might rob them of the time they spend at their dreary business affairs.

For Stendhal, literature was a means of preserving nature. Literature as he understood and practiced it, at least—namely, a pitiless quest for the most apt and briefest possible expression, and a determination to write nothing that wasn't true. Truth is a capricious, unpredictable line. This line Stendhal constantly controlled. He followed its slightest variation with a sensitive finger. Never swerving from it, he never swerved from himself. He was always "in contact" with his own truth, that is to say with what gave or failed to give him happiness— in other words, with nature.

The good writer is a graphomaniac; he needs to write every day, just as cows need to be milked, otherwise their udders begin to ache. The maxim "*Nulla dies sine linea*" is useful in two ways. In the first place, the thread of creation is taut and easily snaps. A day passed without writing interrupts the writer's momentum, destroys a habit and a method; it takes several days of strenuous work to make up for one day of idleness; it takes a multitude of knots to retie the thread. Secondly, a day which doesn't leave one at least one line is a day lost, irremediably buried in futility and oblivion. A day without creation, however slight, might never have existed. It has been struck off without a counterpart in life. To be saved, it would need nothing less than the memory of an extreme happiness.* At twenty-three, Mérimée, already capable of writing *Le Théâtre de Clara Gazul*, wasted an incredible amount of time on fruitless amusements and vain pleasures. This witty young man was widely fêted, and it is delightful to be fêted at twenty-three. I myself enjoyed a little of this (less than Mérimée, of course, having neither his precocity nor his success, nor his background, nor his fortune, nor his brilliant friends); this cost me two or three books which I haven't written, which I shall never write, and which would have been no worse than the rest. Anyway, laziness is always fatal, for it is by writing that one encounters ideas, just as it is by walking that one meets adventures. Work brings its own reward, which is a further dose of work. In other words, inspiration feeds on itself. Every artist knows that method is the mother of fertility and that the copious is better than the rare. Simple arithmetic teaches us that the man who has written fifty books has a better chance of having produced twenty good ones than the man who has written only ten. "The worst man with a pistol," says Musset in *Fantasio*, "can hit the bull's-eye if he fires 780 shots a minute just as successfully as the most skillful man who fires only one or two well-aimed ones." The ideal is naturally to be the skillful man and, at the same time, to fire 780 shots a minute.

But enough of comparisons drawn from ballistics—Cocteau has exhausted them in *Le Secret professionnel*. I can compare the writer quite well to a miner. Every day he goes down to the bottom of the mine without knowing exactly what he will bring back. But his spoils matter little. The vital thing is to have the courage to leave the free air in which normal people breathe and to plunge three hundred feet below ground,

---

* "Had I spoken in 1795 of my project of writing and had some sensible man said to me, 'Write for two hours every day, genius or no genius,' this would have made me spend ten years of my life idiotically waiting for *genius*." (*Brulard*, Chapter 19.)

where he knows there will be nothing but darkness, a foul and oppressive atmosphere, setbacks, deceptions, thankless labor, fatigue and disappointments, not to say despair. The head reels; one works in a sort of suffocating dream, one rips one's hands trying to wrench lumps of coal from the walls of the mine; the finest lumps slip through one's fingers and fall down bottomless pits; one passes rich veins without noticing them. The amazing thing is that one climbs back to the surface feeling very gay and plants beside the hole a little red flag which flutters very proudly at the faintest puff of wind, while every now and then one casts a tender glance at it. No pleasure can compare with working the mine. And little does it matter if one brings back only a speck of dust—the little flag is there to show by its waving that the mine exists. One will go down again tomorrow, and devil take it if one isn't more lucky.

The next day everything has to be begun all over again; one sees only the deep black hole, and the hours of boredom and strain, the mortal solitude, the exhaustion. Why go down, then? Nothing compels one to do so. On the contrary, everything cries out to you to remain on the earth's surface, where the sun is shining, the women are willing and the one thought of your nonmining friends is to soothe your remorse. I don't exaggerate when I say that the writer needs superhuman courage every day to tear himself away from the common round of life and dive into the obscure depths of his soul. Nothing in art is ever acquired. Each morning the artist starts again from scratch.

My mining analogy contradicts what I said above about graphomania and the cow's aching udders. Yet all these things coexist. Anyway, what is a contradiction? We live in perpetual contradiction, and artists more than anyone else. Prometheus loves his vulture; he sees it in the guise of an eagle. From the practical angle, let us say that the method or habit of going down into the mine every day makes things easier. Habit transforms chores into pleasures and pleasures into chores— that is its virtue and its vice.

At any rate, Stendhal, who in his maxims yielded nothing to the most exacting moralist, once again prescribed the most difficult way with his *"Nulla dies . . ."* He regarded literature with the eye of love alone. *"Nulla dies sine linea"* is the maxim of a writer more akin to Werther than to Don Juan. The Wertheresque writer is one whose mind and heart are constantly absorbed in his work, who relates everything to it, who hopelessly pursues it for months and sometimes years. But when the work finally smiles and says to him, "I love you," he feels, like the Duc de Nemours with the Princesse de Clèves, a joy greater than that of Napoleon at Marengo. The Don Juanesque writer, who works by fits and starts, for whom each book is an adventure, each article a passing fancy, "must feel that the humblest general who wins a battle, the humblest prefect who keeps control of a province, enjoys a delight more remarkable than his own."

Bad painters *overpolish*, that is to say they make only surface corrections, they perfect only the details. Good painters correct in depth. So did Stendhal. His alterations affected both the ideas and the structure. His negligences of style were of no more consequence than a slight carelessness in the dress of a man built like Apollo. One finds similar negligences in Rembrandt and even in Poussin. They betoken not lack of skill but contempt for petty detail. Today writers and painters retain the negligences only from the teachings of their great predecessors; art is no longer more or less Apollo clad in a well-cut suit; it is a mollusk without bones or nerves, rigged out in cheap finery clumsily run up by ignorant tailors. In the old days they overpolished, now they merely daub; but it is still a question of detail, the last thing one should worry about in art—something given as a bonus, without entailing work, to serious artists.

To remember an author's ideas without being able to recall how they were worded means that one need attach oneself only to his soul. If the soul is mighty enough, it suffices to model the body. A beautiful soul expresses itself of necessity through a beautiful face; if the face is ugly, it still has magnificent eyes with such an eloquent gaze that one is made to forget the crooked nose and toothless mouth. Balzac, Saint-Simon, Proust, Claudel and Montaigne are covered with cankers, scars, warts and boils, but what eyes! Deep, glittering, filled with an incalculable poetry, they either force you to lower your gaze or absorb your whole attention. It is true that "great thoughts have a style," that this style is enough, that it is adapted to them and that they are born fully adorned with the glamour of fine language. Take Stendhal, who writes like the man who drafted the Civil Code or like a mathematician, always terse, never afraid to repeat the same word a line later, indifferent to traditional or original grace of style: he has one of the most beautiful styles in French literature. His music rivals that of Mozart.

Pascal says that true eloquence derides eloquence, just as true morality derides morality. This again describes Stendhal, but only him and his peers. False eloquence and false morality, in which we are immersed today, have no right to deride ordinary eloquence and morality as they do, for then nothing is left. Degas, appalled by the extravagances of the bourgeois painters of his day, had already cried, *"Les pompiers prennent feu!"** Why, the frozen conventionalists who docilely followed the etiolated principles of traditional eloquence and morality cause me less horror than the incandescent *pompiers* who sent these principles packing, to replace them with their ludicrous ideas and rudimentary instincts. What impertinence!

---

* An untranslatable play on words. Literally, "The firemen are catching fire!"; but *pompier* also means "academic" or "conventionally dull."—Tr.

The *pompiers* of yore were at least modest: they didn't trust in their genius.

Stendhal's contempt for style is that of an aristocrat to whom style was granted at birth, like arms or eyes, and not only so far as writing was concerned. Style was the least of his problems. It wasn't even a problem at all. It is regrettable that all authors don't share this contempt and consider that, if one takes up writing, style is "the least of things." How can one venture on a work of literature when one has no style? This seems to me the height of absurdity or futility. It is more honorable to be a civil engineer or an undertaker, a cobbler or a veterinarian. These callings serve some useful purpose. A writer without style merely serves to put stupid ideas into the heads of good people who had no ideas at all before.

Stendhal's aversion for affectation and pretentiousness, for words that are startling when juxtaposed and for bizarre twists given to trivial thoughts, is analogous to the aversion felt by an honest man for pickpockets, swindlers, con men and cadgers of every description, egregious asses, charlatans, braggarts and so on. Besides, this category of people clutters up the arts in every age, and the contagion of the fashionable style in 1958 is as noxious as it was in 1840. To forget the wording and remember the ideas there must necessarily be ideas. Such a necessity doesn't suit writers who have nothing to say and say it in fifty volumes. To take two "great names," who today remembers the ideas of Gide or Giraudoux? When one thinks of them, one evokes nothing but their mannerisms and tricks of style.

Banality of expression is the most difficult form of art, for it is suited only to powerful or pointed ideas; on these it confers a charm or an extra elegance. To preserve himself from the contagion of the fashionable style, Stendhal's practice of ceaselessly reading our great prose writers of the seventeenth and eighteenth centuries remains a sovereign remedy. Pascal,

Bossuet, Montesquieu, Diderot, Rousseau and even Voltaire are sublime schools of banality.

"He loved reading," says Mérimée. I don't want to conclude this chapter without a word about this. People whose childhood has been supervised, thwarted, constrained, who were little slaves like Beyle, almost always love reading, for they have conquered it in its time. Children who have the misfortune not to share any of their family's feelings or ideas pounce on books as prisoners do on sleep, in order to escape the miseries of their lives. Their living masters having proved worthless, they seek dead masters who advise them and, tacitly, approve of them.* It is by way of books that one finds one's world, one's spiritual home. Stendhal found his thanks to Saint-Simon, Helvétius and Montesquieu. "Thenceforward, stealing books became my one aim," he writes in *Brulard*. This note refers to about his seventh year. A man whose one aim at seven was to steal books in order to feast on them in secret remains an ardent lover of reading all his life.

Just as it is bad and sterilizing for a writer to read the mass of second-rate authors of his day, it is also beneficial to read and reread the good authors of the past. They are the hormones necessary for the development of talent. A great writer is always well read. Those who claim that they "never read anything" are the victims of an incomprehensible affectation.

For myself, I felt from the earliest age a sense of amazement over and an appetite for books which have never been sated. I don't think I have passed a day without taking some nourishment from a book. Those who declare that they "never have time to read" astound me. There is always time to read. Every day brings moments of relaxation—fifteen minutes here, half

---

* "Reading *La Nouvelle Héloïse*, and the scruples of Saint-Preux, turned me into a profoundly honest man. . . . Thus it was a book read in great secrecy and against my parents' will which made me an honest man." (*Brulard*.)

an hour there—during which one can enrich one's mind at little cost. Reading is a fountain of youth; those who neglect it age quickly. But one must approach books with complete simplicity. Fools, who are never simple, distrust novels. Worthier souls, even if they lack experience, sense that good authors do not lie. If one reads Balzac with the same faith as a scientific treatise, it can save one ten years of floundering or mistakes.

For a young man sensitive to beauty, ready to learn from his superiors, endowed with the taste artists have for rather outlandish and extravagant ideas, nothing is more beneficial than to plunge headlong into reading. The good French authors are the best of teachers. They will train him to think clearly; they will give him a distaste for facile mystery, a contempt for muddled and confused ideas and, finally, a writer's confidence in the French language which precludes all equivocation. Rivarol, in his *Discours sur l'universalité de la langue française*, which I admire in spite of the scorn of modern philologists, says, "The French language is the only one that has an integrity allied to its genius." This integrity perforce worms its way into the reader's mind. French is the only language in the world which forms an education and a method for the mind, not through what it expresses but through the way in which it expresses it. One becomes simple through familiarity with the French classics. The glance one subsequently casts on life reflects this. It is the glance of a gentleman of the seventeenth or eighteenth century. But one's judgment is none the worse for being two hundred years behind the times. Good sense and intelligence are ageless. Montesquieu goes deeper than the fashionable thinkers of today. As for new ideas, they are quickly learned; one merely has to skim through a newspaper.

For him, poetry was a closed book. He would often murder verses when reciting them. Although he spoke a pure and fluent Italian and knew English pretty well, he understood neither the meter nor the stresses of English and Italian poetry. However, he had a feeling for certain beauties in Shakespeare and Dante which are closely bound up with the form of the verse. He said his last word on poetry in his book De l'Amour: *"Verses were invented to aid the memory; to preserve them in dramatic art is a relic of barbarism." He had a supreme dislike of Racine. The great fault of which he accused Racine in 1820 was that he was totally lacking in* mores, *or what, in our Romantic jargon, we used to call* local color. *Shakespeare, whom we always held up in contrast to Racine, had faults a hundred times more glaring in this respect, which we were careful not to mention. "But," Beyle used to say, "Shakespeare knew the human heart better. There is no passion, no emotion he did not paint with wonderful truth, in all its shades. The vitality and inimitable individuality of all his characters set him above all other dramatists." "And Molière," we would reply, "where do you rank him?" "Molière was a rogue who didn't want to stage* Le Courtisan *because Louis XIV thought it was a bad play."*

WHAT DOES Mérimée mean by saying that poetry was "a closed book"? What could be more poetic than *La Chartreuse de Parme* in its language, its development, its details and its music? I am afraid that Mérimée here was confusing poetry and versification, or even poetry and bombast. In Stendhal's paradoxes I discern above all the spirit of contradiction, for which poetry is a chosen domain. Indeed, nothing is so intolerable to a man of taste as the extravagances of the bad, and even the good, poets of his time. Stendhal nevertheless conceded that Lamartine had written two hundred beautiful lines, which is not so far from the mark. He made fun of Victor Hugo when the occasion arose, but never very wholeheartedly. Hugo was forty when Stendhal died; he had not yet produced his best work. I am convinced that Stendhal would have adored *Les Châtiments*, gone mad over *Le Cimetière d'Eylau*, been enchanted by *La Légende des siècles* and loved *La Fin de Satan* as much as his dear Dante.

What was a "closed book" for him was a certain type of poetry, a certain fashionable tone in poetry to which he had taken a dislike when he was eighteen because at that age, if one has temperament or genius, one hates anything that is different from oneself or that reminds one of a few childish errors of taste for which one still blushes. "At seventeen," says Stendhal, "I nearly fought a duel over Chateaubriand's *cime indéterminée des forêts*, which counted many admirers in the Sixth Dragoons." At seventeen I hadn't the good fortune to be in the Sixth Dragoons with the army in Italy. I was at the Lycée Janson de Sailly in Paris; but, like Stendhal, I nearly fought a duel—over Gide's *Nathanaël*, which had many fans in the philosophy class and which got on my nerves. "Since most rogues are bombastic and eloquent," he also says, "one soon develops a hatred for the declamatory style." Alas, what optimism from a perceptive man like Beyle! There are always rogues to declaim and gullible fools to cry that this is poetry. It is a daily feature of our lives in 1958. "Rogue" must be taken in its widest sense, ranging from the simple con man to government leaders and the professors of noble sentiments in the patriotic or defeatist press. In my youth I felt the same mistrust of poetry as Stendhal. I was not unaware that an eloquent style often conceals an arid soul, and that the truly eloquent soul prefers to express itself in a dry style.

Lyricism is so often hollow and insincere that if, at seventeen, one has anything like an honest and rational mind and a sensitive heart, one develops a horror of it for the rest of one's life. Beyle, as a little boy, suffered much from his father Chérubin's and his Aunt Séraphie's hypocritical admiration of the country around Grenoble and the sunsets over Furonières. When he was seventeen, France was infatuated with *Atala*, which is by far the worst thing Chateaubriand ever wrote. The sunsets on the Meschacebé must have irritated him as much as those on the Drac. He must have seen the same exaggerated and false light in both of them. We today tackle Chateaubriand through the *Mémoires d'Outretombe*, a great work, and no longer read *Atala*. In 1801 the *Mémoires* were not even begun. In 1842 they had not been published.

Stendhal found himself at the confluence of two streams of poetry: that of the eighteenth century, withered, insipid, dull, mummified in classicism, and that of the early nineteenth century, full of audacity and flatulence. To him we owe the justly famous remark, "The Alexandrine is often merely a means of concealing stupidity." Certainly the phrase Mérimée quotes from *De l'Amour* is not that of a poet, but neither is it that of an enemy of poetry. At most, the remark of an antiversifier, perhaps of a man who remembers *Le Jardin des racines grecques** with disgust. For a hundred years—from 1700 to 1800—apart from Chénier, France had been handing out proof that one can make millions of rhymes without an ounce of poetry. The converse is equally true. The poets of 1958, who

* A collection of rhyming verses designed to help one memorize Greek roots and used by generations of French schoolchildren.—Tr.

do not make rhymes, are no more poets than Lebrun or Florian. They don't even take the trouble to conceal their imbecilities in Alexandrines.

Stendhalian poetry, which is intense and dramatic, almost always derives from *privileged circumstances,* whether these concern the author or his characters: the view of Lake Garda, the chiming of a bell on the hillside half a mile above Rolle or Nyon, Sorel throwing himself into the arms of the Abbé Pirard, and so on. This last scene is so poetic that it hardly ever fails to draw tears to the eyes as one reads it; but let there be no mistake—it is the beauty that brings the tears, not what happens. The marvelous thing about Stendhal, by which one recognizes the poet in him, is that the situations are always privileged, never indifferent. In *Lucien Leuwen,* for instance, I estimate there are several hundred privileged situations, which make this novel a poem as complete as *Orlando Furioso.* All this poetry is expressed in terse and pithy sentences, without emphasis and with abrupt endings; it comes to us across the centuries, not like the dried and scentless flowers of the fabricators of odes, but like a concentration of perfume. These are the peaks the Civil-Code style can attain when applied to the emotions. Who would deny that there is a thousand times more poetry in *La Chartreuse,* by this "freethinker," than in *Les Misérables,* the work of a great poet?

I know what they mean when they accuse a writer of not being a poet: they reproach him for being clear, for not making mysteries, for recoiling from the preposterous. And it is true that these qualities, in a second-rate mind, exclude a certain kind of poetry. But in Stendhal the clarity is always sublime. It does not lie on this side of the mysteries, but beyond them. As for the preposterous, he attains this quite easily through logic. The death of Julien Sorel furnishes, in my view, the model of preposterousness made sublime.

Whatever faith I have in Mérimée, I can't believe that Beyle, an artist in all things, murdered verses when he recited them, involuntarily put eleven syllables where there should be twelve, and so on. He had as far as it is possible that special literary ear which is not the same as a musical ear, and thanks to which one can't be mistaken over the polish of a style. The music of words has its own subtle and unwritten laws, which are not those of the music of sounds and which men with a vocation for writing know without having to learn them. One page of Stendhal is enough to prove that he had an infallible ear, and that everything on it is harmonized, even the negligences. It is by their negligences that one recognizes great men, for not any kind of negligence will do. There is an art in negligence, the first condition of which is to know what is important and what is not.

35

Beyle wrote extensively on the fine arts and had ideas of his own at a time when everybody accepted the falsest opinions without question, provided they were sanctioned by a famous author. He might be said to have discovered Rossini and Italian music. His contemporaries will recall the attacks he had to endure in his defense of the composer of The Barber of Seville *and* Semiramis *against the then habitués of the Opéra Comique. During the early years of the Restoration, memory of our reverses had stung our national pride and every dispute was turned into a question of patriotism. To prefer foreign to French music was tantamount to betraying the country. Very early Beyle had set himself above vulgar prejudices, and on this score he sometimes perhaps exceeded his aim. Today, when civilization has made such progress, it is hard to appreciate the courage it took in 1818 to say that some Italian opera was better than some French one. One has to hark back to the great quarrels between Romanticism and Classicism to find an explanation for the roundabout precautions with which Beyle dressed up some of his judgments on artistic matters. Bold and even rash when he published them, they now seem glimpses of the obvious,* truisms, *according to their author's favorite expression.*

WHAT IDEAS would Stendhal have had on art, what positions would he have taken up if, in 1818, our reverses, instead of exasperating national pride, had simply obliterated it, as happened between 1945 and 1958? I think the spirit of contradiction would have played just as great a part, but in the opposite sense. When France is in a chauvinistic and swaggering mood, one feels an overwhelming desire to insult her. When she denigrates herself, humiliates, belittles and slanders herself, one can't resist hymning all her merits, and even inventing them for her. I know these reactions, having had the first in 1938 and the second in 1950.

Ideas, or positions, are not stupid in themselves. What is stupid is the use to which they are put. So long as ideas remain the appanage of a small number of intelligent people, they preserve all their power by the mere fact that their expression is not foolish. When they become public property, the entertainers, professional interpreters and popularizers take them over, simplify them to an extreme, illustrate them with facile examples and turn them to any and every use. They become intolerant and intolerable. What one had opted for of one's own free will becomes obligatory. All conformity is odious, because it presupposes approval of principles simplified to such an extent that the greatest number may understand and adopt them. "Vulgar prejudice" follows a sinusoidal curve. That of 1818 had completely disappeared in 1950 and, having been replaced by the inverse prejudice, became the prerogative of the happy few.

Whatever its object, the stupidity is the same. Even so, one feels more at ease fighting intolerant patriotism than antipatriotism. I envy Stendhal for having happened on a period of fanatical and bigoted patriotism. Today even the most complete idiot will tell you that art has no nationality and beauty scorns frontiers. What can you reply to that? The idiot is right, obviously, but he is wrong to be right. They are bad reasons which have led him to this truth. A truth deduced from a string of lies is merely an additional lie.

The spirit of contradiction springs from three praiseworthy emotions: a desire for justice, as I have said before; courage, for it takes this to uphold a viewpoint counter to that of public opinion; and intellectual probity, for no thoughtful or at all subtle mind could ever accept the oversimplified and provocative appeal that fashionable ideas always assume. The man afflicted with a spirit of contradiction is the opposite of a fanatic, he is objective; whether he admires or disapproves, his words and actions tend to "put things in their proper place."

In his discovery of Rossini and Italian music, and his dogged defense of them against the *habitués* of the Opéra Comique, Stendhal shows himself in his usual light. He extols what he loves, and all the more openheartedly the more public opinion disapproves of it. One takes a similar delight today in maintaining that Giraudoux is crumbling to dust, that Tchaikovsky is a "palm court" composer, that Béatrix Beck and Bernard Frank are more talented than the accepted geniuses of the avant-garde, and so on. Today these opinions may seem bold and even rash. In twenty or thirty years' time they in turn will be "truisms."

Such is the unhappy fate of the critic. He loses either way: when he is wrong, he is forgotten; when, at the cost of bitter persecution, he dares to be clear-sighted, posterity disdainfully says that he merely did his duty and that there is no great merit in that.

There was no great merit, we think today, in preferring Rossini (who was anyway not a very great man) to the concocters of French light operas in the year 1818. Rossini is a charming composer, deft, gay, inventive, prolific, immeasurably superior to what one could hear under the Restoration. In 1832, by which time Rossini was recognized, Stendhal wrote in his *Souvenirs d'égotisme*, "The Chevalier had retained the art of accompanying on the piano superlatively well and enough musical good sense or good taste, whichever you prefer, not to be completely taken in by Rossini's whipped cream and flashiness." See how the spirit of contradiction re-establishes the truth and provides fair judgments!

36 *Without being a musician, Beyle had a very keen sense of melody, cultivated and perfected by a certain erudition which he owed to his travels in Italy and Germany. In music, to my mind, what he loved and sought above all were dramatic effects or, rather, when analyzing his personal impressions he explained these by means of dramatic language, the only one he knew or believed to be intelligible to his readers.*

THERE ARE two ways of discussing the arts: as a technician or as a man of sensibility. Beyle discussed literature as a technician. Since he was not a virtuoso where the other arts were concerned, he judged these only with his heart, as a civilized man and not as a pedant. The following passage from *Brulard* shows that he was also capable of translating dramatic language into music:

> In the heyday of my taste for music, in Milan between 1814 and 1821, when I used to fetch my libretto from the Scala on the morning of a new opera, I couldn't prevent myself as I read it from composing all its music, from singing its arias and duets. And dare I say it? Sometimes that evening I would find my own melody *nobler* and *more tender* than that of the maestro.

There are numerous examples of great artists taking an interest in arts other than the one at which they excel. In fact, the paths of all the arts are alike and each art, through its own path, heads toward the common goal. "Nothing which has to do with art is alien to me," every genuine artist may say when he is twenty. The expression "the family of the arts" signifies something: a painter feels himself the brother or cousin of a composer or a poet of the same breed. Only the language keeps them apart. Let an interpreter appear and they realize that they think the same way about everything. Why do I say an interpreter? They are polyglots. But one naturally speaks one's mother tongue best. Stendhal translated music and painting at sight into what Mérimée calls dramatic language. He gives an excellent description of the joy to be had from music, for the supreme intention of art for the amateur is to procure a certain measure of joy. "Good music never errs," says Stendhal, "but goes straight to the depths of the soul to seek out the sorrow that devours us."

It is perhaps important to know that Beyle, when young, thought he had a vocation for music. Psychoanalysts say that children up to fifteen or sixteen are indiscriminately attracted by both sexes and that there are no clearly defined homosexuals or heterosexuals. Something similar takes place in the mind of an artist: all the arts attract him until finally one of them wins the day. "Chance," says Stendhal in *Brulard*, "willed it that I should seek to record the sounds of my soul through the printed page. Laziness and lack of opportunity to learn the physical, mechanical side of music—namely, how to play the piano and note down my ideas—played a large part in this decision, which might have been quite different had I found an uncle or mistress who loved music. As for the passion, that remained complete."

Chance is exactly the right word. At twenty, if I may be allowed to compare my humble experiences with those of Stendhal, I experienced a similar stroke of chance. I was a painter; I thought painting was my most serious vocation, although I was equally curious about music and poetry. I painted and I wrote. One day I had to choose between these two arts toward which I was so strongly drawn and for which I believe I was equally gifted. Chance and nothing else guided my choice. I, too, had rather neglected the physical, mechanical side of painting. I had neither uncle nor mistress to encourage me; I had not three or four years of serious study of anatomy and composition behind me. And I almost blush to give my final reason, it is so frivolous; but it shows how strong is the part played by chance in the gravest decisions: I gave up painting chiefly because of the materials (brushes, paints, canvases, easels, etc.) which it requires. "Writing is much more simple and comfortable," I told myself. "All one needs is a pad of paper and a pen. And one can write anywhere: sitting on a stone or a crate, in a prison or a café. Whereas painting . . ." Such are the motives through which one radically alters one's life; chance willed it that I should seek to record the colors and shapes of my soul through the printed page. I am convinced that certain people will take me severely to task and accuse me of being petty and mean. For a long time I myself felt ashamed at not having abandoned painting for nobler reasons and I kept the true reason for my choice a secret. This was stupid; nothing is as beautiful as the truth, nothing is as pleasing.

Stendhal says something which goes a bit further than the translation of music into dramatic language: "Does music appeal to me as a *symbol*, a memory of the joys of youth, or *in itself?*" And he adds, "I favor the second reason." In other words, he was a connoisseur, an enlightened amateur who, contrary to what Mérimée says, did not seek in art a pretext for allegories but savored its essence, went straight to the irreducible kernel, the "profound song," which means nothing precisely but signifies everything. There is in the *Souvenirs d'égotisme* a profound passage which shows that Stendhal understood music better than the professionals: "In Italy I could discuss music with old Mayer, young Pacini and the composers. The performers, the Marquis Carafa, Viscontini of Milan, found on the other hand that I was lacking in common sense. It was just as if I were talking politics today with a subprefect." There are people, in effect, who can talk politics only with ministers, although they have never played any part in the Administration or been deputies.

The way in which Stendhal loved music and the arts in general must be almost incomprehensible today (as it doubtless was in his own time). Nothing is rarer today than "men of sensibility" when it comes to music or painting. Even so, I think that pedantry where art is concerned has progressed since 1830. The countless reviews, filled with technical details on the drawing of the hands in the Master of Moulins, Bonington's brushwork, Turner's sixteen different yellows, the various periods of Wedgwood china, Schoenberg's "musical breathing" and so on, go to prove it. These publications, which interest *really* only about two hundred people, are very prosperous and sometimes luxurious. They are bought not by the men of sensibility but by the most conceited kind of bourgeois because art is smart, just as if they were buying industrial or colonial magazines.

One should not unreservedly accept Beyle's fleeting, whimsical and inconsequential tastes simply because he is Stendhal. In music he loved melody at the expense of harmony, just as in literature he was preoccupied only with ideas. Unfortunately, this is only one half of music. Beautiful melodies certainly have a style, and bad composers have only style without melody. But a melody is nothing without harmony, which takes up and develops the themes; it is just an "air." Albinoni is not superior to Beethoven. Thanks to Stravinsky and his skill, *"Elle avait une jambe de bois"* becomes one of the most delightful motifs in *Petrouchka* and indeed in all modern music.

The melody, like the idea, has to be worked on; in other words, every facet of it has to be examined.

Today, I think that melody is out of favor. Only technique is admired—this is the other half; and music remains just as incomplete. Johann Sebastian Bach, whom people are so mad about just now, is fine only when his work has melody; after all, it is in melody that genius lies. The rest of the time, in his icily arithmetical compositions, he is mortally dull. Bacchic frenzy is one of the characteristics of our contemporary pedants. Everyone lays claim to knowing music, but almost no one yields to its sweetness, its joys, its raptures. People go to concerts the way they go to stare at electronic machines. Alain has said, "I am close to regarding as a monster the man who would read a novel to find out how that novel was put together." When one isn't a performer or composer oneself, and one listens to music to find out how it is put together, one is a monster. The concert halls teem with such monsters, stuffed full of pedantry and totally alien to art.

37 *It was the same with the graphic arts. A passionate admirer of the great masters of the Roman, Florentine and Lombard schools, he often credited them with dramatic intentions which, to my mind, were quite alien to them. When he discovered in a Madonna by Raphael or Correggio, his preferred master, a host of passions or intimations of passion which painting could never truly express, one wondered if he really understood the intentions and the aims of these great masters. But he expressed in his own way the emotions he felt before their works; he described their effect for want of ability to explain its cause. Had he tried at different times to write down his impressions of the same picture, he himself would probably have been surprised by their variety.*

Like all critics, Beyle struggled against a probably insoluble difficulty. Neither our langauge nor any other that I know can describe the qualities of a work of art with exactitude. It is rich enough to distinguish the colors; but, between two shades which have a specific name, how many others are there, perceptible to our eyes but absolutely impossible to define in words! The poverty of language becomes even more apparent when it is a question of forms, no longer one of colors. A moderately trained eye can easily recognize a faulty outline. Anyone who examines the statuette of the Venus de Milo reduced by the Collas process immediately recognizes that the nose is not antique. Yet the difference between this reduced nose and the nose of the Greek sculptor can be only a fraction of a millimeter; now, what words could characterize this form whose beauty depends on a fraction of a millimeter more or less? What is felt so easily cannot be expressed in black and white, *as Beyle used to say.*

This impossibility to be precise has given rise to the need to find terms of comparison which are hardly suited to shed any light on so obscure a problem. The dramatic side in the arts is what we Frenchmen understand best, and it is probably for this reason that Beyle explained beauty through passion. Despite his claims to be a cosmopolitan, he was completely French, both in mind and in heart.

BAD ACTORS exaggerate shades of feeling, speak too loudly or too softly, frown to simulate anger or laugh heartily to suggest irony. Good actors, even when they put on a declamatory tone of voice to play tragedy, preserve a certain impassivity, a certain indifference. Like M. Teste,* who never emphasized his remarks with any gesture, they have "killed the marionette in them." Far from giving the spectacle of puppets agitated by fleeting passions or ephemeral desires without past or future, they embody real, true, opaque, solid characters, whose words are the expression of a soul formed through the years.

What I say of the actor also concerns life. Real tragedies act themselves out in the language of Racine. There is never any blood on the stage, never any passion on the faces. Everything lies behind. Joy is not marked by exuberance, nor despair by tears. On the contrary, one often sees sad joys and despairs full of gaiety. It is through such dissembling, moreover, that one recognizes souls of superior quality. There is nothing so common as to make a spectacle of oneself, and nothing seems so vain as a man who yields without restraint to the promptings of his heart, who passes in a brief space of

---

* A character invented by Paul Valéry.—TR.

time from indignation to smiles and from smiles to melancholy. Here is a soul turned inside out like a rabbitskin, without mystery and therefore without poetry. Besides, this succession of quick changes conveys a cruel impression of nothingness. What is this molecule riddled with passions, who is happy, unhappy, then happy again, and so on ad infinitum? It makes an unbearable caricature of the human condition. It underlines its frailty; it reminds one of the billions of beings who have gone before it, who by turns have similarly suffered and rejoiced and of whom not even a memory remains.

Great works of art have an air of stupidity. This disconcerts people of uncertain or still unformed taste. I was greatly struck by it when I was young, in painting, particularly in portraits. At fourteen I couldn't account for this air of stupidity. I took it to be an inability on the part of the painter to render emotions such as pride, tenderness, joy or sorrow. The following year I understood that the great painters reproduce not the moment, that is to say the more or less fleeting movements of men's hearts, but their permanent state, their constant potential. Hence the calm, almost inexpressive faces, full of mystery—in short, stupid—which people their works. Just as white is the sum of all colors, so a good portrait expresses all the emotions of its sitter, his past and his future; this excludes those transitory upheavals, those dramatic climaxes which make faces interesting. The inner life barely modifies the surface of the flesh. It is merely a light, a reflection. The painter perceives this reflection with his sensibility, with his heart; he translates it with his hand. It can happen that his mind plays no part in this, that the genius passes directly from his heart into his hand without being relayed through his consciousness, which explains and elucidates. But it is also rare for a great painter not to understand, during or after the act, what he wished to do and what he has done.

Painting can express quite clearly a host of passions or intimations of passions, but it expresses them globally, syn-thetically and with its own means, which are not those of literature. Reason is analytical; therefore it uses a dramatic language. Everything must be translated into this language. A fanciful translation, says Mérimée, when Stendhal puts paint-ing into words. I can find no explanation for this mistrust. It gives offense to both Stendhal and his painters. One could not possibly doubt the sincerity of the former any more than the art of the latter. Why should the first be mistaken as to the in-tentions and aims of the second? I don't believe that Stendhal, had he tried at different times to write down his impressions of the same picture, would have been surprised by their va-riety. On the contrary, he would have found the same impres-sions, with ten years between them, for the picture served him in a sense as a notebook. These notes were precise and copious. Instead of being written in black and white, they took the form of a look, a gesture, the curve of a mouth, a fold of drapery. Owing to its precision, this language, although not "dramatic," precludes any ambiguity. The artist's aim is to reproduce nature, heightened by the poetry peculiar to the look which seizes it and the hand which pins it down. Stendhal, endowed with extreme sensibility and perception, recognized unfailingly both the nature and the poetry.

Here is a conclusive example. When for the first time I read the account Stendhal gives of Leonardo's "Last Supper" in Chapter 45 of his *Histoire de la peinture en Italie*, I did not feel the slightest surprise; here, down to the last detail, were my ideas, my own ideas and feelings about this fresco. What can Mérimée reply to that? Between Stendhal's impressions and mine more than 130 years have elapsed, and two different people are concerned. Love what you will never see twice, cries Vigny in a truly pathetic outburst, for the most desper-ate thing in life is never to be able to enjoy the same happi-ness twice over. On the other hand, the work of art, which is eternally identical to itself and which can be seen a hundred, a thousand times, consoles man for his despair. One finds it there, unchanged, as often as one wishes to revive, equally unchanged, the emotions one has long forgotten. Works of art are landmarks, immobile monuments in the midst of passing life. That, among other things, is what Stendhal illustrates and what Mérimée rather irresponsibly denies.

Anyway, everything in this critical passage of Mérimée's strikes me as debatable, and even worse: short-sighted or narrow. Weren't they in 1850 already talking of "expressing the inexpressible"? But Mérimée was a wise man for whom the inexpressible did not constitute a literary subject. I suppose that to him the inexpressible, in Théophile Gautier's sense, seemed the simplest thing in the world to express, and therefore didn't merit any declarations of principle. The genuinely inexpressible, for a work of art, is another work of art; for one art, another art. At least it was in 1850. For after that came Proust, who contrives to make his reader *hear* Vinteuil's famous septet.

Stendhal practiced art criticism like Diderot: he described pictures, and he interlarded his descriptions with impressions of joy, happiness or sadness as he felt them. Proust doesn't describe Vinteuil's septet any differently; he metamorphoses this music into so poetic and highly colored a description that one thinks of a picture, but a picture that would unfold (however incomprehensible this may seem) at once in space and time, that would combine plasticity and continuance. Stendhal also plays on space and time when he transposes painting. "Dramatic language" is clearly indispensable to this operation. Proust uses it in the same way as Stendhal. "He makes music accessible through ideas." Contrary to what Mérimée maintains, the "terms of comparison" are perfectly fitted to shed light on this obscure problem. Where does the term of comparison end and the metaphor begin? The latter is the instrument of the poet; with this he expresses the inexpressible, like a mathematician of the emotions reducing a new problem to an already demonstrated proposition.

Stendhal is as close to Baudelaire as to Diderot, through his predilection for ideas, through his aesthetic theories, his bird's-eye view of the works and general notions on the artists he is concerned with. Through taste, finally. Reading Diderot, one cannot in fact help thinking that one is dealing with a critic from the provinces, and that his salon was not in Paris but in Langres, with a group of regional painters. There is nothing like this in Stendhal, whose artistic horizon is infinitely wider and who, like Baudelaire, probes into souls truly worthy of his own with open eyes, quick to pounce on every detail, however unflattering.

Dare I say that I find the part about the Venus de Milo's nose and the fraction of a millimeter quite preposterous and beside the point? It is a question not of describing this nose by fractions of a millimeter but of conveying the fraction of a millimeter in words, possibly in metaphors. I have already said that the arts resemble each other. If one wants to find the equivalent of the Venus' nose in Stendhal's work, it is enough to read two paragraphs from *La Chartreuse*. Any delicate emotion of Fabrice or his aunt corresponds perfectly to its exquisite and inimitable curve. This reasoning is subtle, and perhaps incomprehensible to the bourgeois, but artists or people with any knowledge of an art will understand it instantly.

To describe the effect of a picture without being able to explain its cause, to express in one's own way the emotions it arouses, is the natural procedure for a man of sensibility and the converse of that of the pedant. The latter seeks the cause without heeding the effect; this is to prefer objectivity to truth. Truth is first and foremost the truth of oneself. And what is the "cause" in a picture? It consists of lines, dabs of paint, a whole irrational mechanism whose one aim is to provoke emotions in the spectator's soul. If the latter is very highly tuned and sensitive, it approaches till it meets the soul of the great painter it admires. Mérimée forgets that painting, like all the arts, is a means of communication. A combination of lines and colors is like a combination of words or sounds. Their arrangement tends to produce an effect. Analysis of this effect is more important than analysis of its cause. Through this one can work back to the cause and perceive the secrets of how genius operates.

It is untrue that painters have no dramatic intentions. Pictures representing some legendary or historic scene, such as "The Wedding at Cana" or "The Death of Sardanapalus," are great immobile dramas or petrified operas. The art of painting consists in showing simultaneously the beginning, the climax and the decline—in other words, in giving in one instant the feeling of duration. This is achieved only thanks to a certain permanence in the expression of the faces (whence their air of stupidity) and a highly developed skill in the general composition, through the harmony of which a moment in time is captured for all eternity. This is what Stendhal, although he does not formally express it, always felt keenly and knew how to translate in his descriptions of emotions. This brings us back to "The Last Supper," which, in this sense, is a model of sensibility.

"The dramatic side in the arts is what we Frenchmen understand best." This is a profound remark. It redeems the paragraph. It is true that we best grasp the complexities of men's souls by illustration of the facts. That is the propensity of the French, as opposed to the Scandinavian or Germanic, mind. Facts leave no room for ambiguity; one can weigh them and, having done so, deduce with greater precision the movement of the soul which has given rise to them. Here again one proceeds from the effect to the cause, and the sensitive soul merges with the logical (or rationalist) soul. A blend which might well have been designed to please Stendhal.

38

He seemed to me to be much less sensitive to sculpture than to painting. Antique statues struck him as being too lacking in passion, and he accused them of giving the impression of beautiful but witless beings. His favorite sculptor was Canova, whose grace he admired whilst admitting that it was a trifle mannered. I think that he praised Michelangelo more highly than he actually cared for him. When he took me to see his Moses *on the tomb of Julius II, he found no way to commend it to me other than to say that the expression of inflexible ferocity could not be better rendered.*

REGARDING Stendhal's admiration for Canova, the reader should turn back to page 67. It is also interesting to set Mérimée's text against the following lines from *L'Histoire de la peinture en Italie* referring to the "Moses" (Chapter 164):

"Unless you have seen this statue, you do not know all the powers of sculpture. Modern sculpture is of little account. I imagine that, if it had to compete with the Greeks, it would present a dancer by Canova and the 'Moses.' The Greeks would be astonished to see things so new and with such powerful effects on the human heart." Stendhal adds, "One of the joys of this statue is the singular kinship which chance brought about between the character of the artist and that of the prince." For prince, read Pope Julius II, who had commissioned the "Moses." It is rare indeed, in the history of patronage, to find two such equally lofty and unyielding spirits meeting and pleasing each other in the way that Julius II and Michelangelo did. It represents a sort of brotherhood of ogres which must have delighted Stendhal (and also delights me). In such unions the fools, intriguers and mediocrities have everything to fear. Strength, combined with intellect and genius, leads to a ferocious dictatorship and an even more intolerable scorn.

It is amusing that Stendhal could find nothing to reply to Mérimée other than what the latter reports. He doesn't say much more in his Chapter 164. The fact is that sometimes the constructive analysis of beauty is discouraging. Besides, Beyle was quite the opposite of a pedagogue. One cannot picture him as a lecturer at the school of the Louvre, expounding the most obvious qualities of the best-known masterpieces to a handful of imbeciles who are "doing" art as they would do Latin. Stendhal leaves out everything that is self-evident to any cultivated man. Did Mérimée expect a lecture on Michelangelo, his power, his modeling, and so on? Such things are taken for granted; they are ignored, in order to go straight to what is essential or remarkable in a work. The remarkable, the unexpected thing about the "Moses" is its air of inflexible ferocity. Beyle, as a freethinker, as a Voltairian, also recalled the succession of crimes and deeds of violence with which the Old Testament and the history of the Hebrew people are studded; through Moses, he was making a slight joke against the Bible. A joke tempered by admiration, for he infinitely relished the inflexible ferocity of the great spirits of the Renaissance. But enough of these subtleties.

"One thing instantly destroys antique beauty: its air of inanity." This remark, in Chapter 86 of *L'Histoire de la peinture en Italie,* illustrates Stendhal's method: to trust in one's sensibility and express it bluntly. If one doesn't attain the truth, at least one attains one's own truth, which almost always amounts to the same thing. To trust in all matters to one's sensibility is equivalent to turning one's back on centuries of commonplaces.

I apologize for returning to the story of the Emperor's new clothes, but the man of sensibility is like the little boy who exclaimed, "His Majesty is naked!" and accordingly either provoked the people's wrath or opened their eyes. Stendhal's eyes saw all the emperors, even the most respectable and revered, in their nakedness. For Stendhal, truth had no more moral significance than a landscape or a jug. The landscape and the jug must be represented as they are. One must "capture their likeness." Nothing is more absurd and contemptible than those people who travesty the truth because of small contingent intentions, or out of snobbery, or in order to embellish, or simply to conform. The truth is an absolute; it doesn't alter because twenty generations either fail to recognize it or flout it. The inane appearance of antique beauty is an incontestable truth.* Even today this assertion startles millions of sheep who have learned what they feel from books on art history written by people who have no understanding of art. Stendhal was an uncompromising man. He calmly stated the most unpopular ideas. Calmly, because they were perfectly obvious to this mind, at once so simple and so profound.

---

* This air of inanity is not to be confused with the air of stupidity to be found in great works. The latter is due to the concentration of passion; it is white—the sum of all colors. The air of inanity is due to the absence of passion; it is black, which is no color at all.

39 *Beyle set little store by the colorists. We used to have long arguments about it. He thoroughly despised Rubens and his school; he took the Flemish and even the Venetians to task for the triviality of their forms and their poverty of expression. Correggio, according to Beyle, had combined to a supreme degree perfection of form with the art of aerial perspective. For him, Correggio was the most pleasing painter and Michelangelo the most poetically terrible.*

STENDHAL finds analogies between the art of Correggio on the one hand and literature and music on the other. In his *Journal*, under the date March 5, 1812, he writes, "Who would have told me that I should dislike the *Confessions* of J.-J. Rousseau and that I should look for color in Fénelon? The drawing of Télémaque* is, in truth, pitiful, but it is his coloring which seems to me to come closest to Allegri."

Artistic sensibility likes to compare the masters of different arts with each other, to detect in what ways a painter is the replica of some poet or musician, how they express the same thing, the same soul, by different means. Stendhal excelled at this game and loved to play it. This implies a "resonant" soul, which perceives the profound song of the creative artist through the forms this song assumes, recognizing the same sounds in painting, the same colors in music.

---

* In *Les Aventures de Télémaque*, a famous novel by Fénelon.—TR.

I see I am talking a great deal about soul in this book. But it is about Stendhal, and there is almost nothing but soul in the whole of this atheist's work. To hear music when one looks at painting is more a matter of soul than of taste. This means that before the spectacle of the arts one feels not the *aesthetic pleasure* of which the pundits speak so coldly, but *joy*. The more sensitive the soul, the better it recognizes this joy when it appears. Art is merely its vehicle. In fact, it is the absorbing dialogue between one lofty soul and another which it places on its own level. Certainly, Fénelon and Correggio speak more or less the same language; but I should be hard put to it to explain why. This identity is clear only to sensitive souls, who have no need of explanation.

In Chapter 28 of his *Histoire de la peinture en Italie*, Stendhal talks of Poussin's landscapes, which set the soul dreaming. "It feels itself transported into these noble vistas, and to find there that happiness which eludes us in reality." This idea is accompanied by a few reflections which I shall take the liberty of quoting in full, for fear of misrepresenting them by a paraphrase. (Besides, I can't help feeling that, the more Stendhal I quote, the pleasanter this book will be! I prefer his prose to mine. While writing this book, I keep comparing myself to the music commentators on the radio who plague us until we say, "Why do they go on so? Why don't they shut up and let us hear their records?") Here is the passage:

The magic of distances, that part of painting which beguiles tender imaginations, is perhaps the principal reason for its superiority to sculpture. By this means it comes close to music, it enlists the imagination to complete its pictures. . . . [The art of Correggio] was to paint even the foreground figures as if they were in the distance. Out of every twenty people they captivate, there is perhaps not one who sees them, and above all remembers them, in the same way. This is music and it is not sculpture. One aches to enjoy it more positively; one would like to touch these figures—*Quis enim modus adsit amori!* But it is through too close an acquaintance that our hearts grow weary of the things they have loved best: immense advantage of music, which passes by like human activities. *O debolezza dell'uom, o natura nostra mortale!* Divine emotions can exist here on earth only so long as they are brief.

It is one of the secrets of the sensitive soul that it thrives in the borderlands of the arts, in the places where they meet and intermingle. Stendhal hunted happiness in every field—love, painting, music, nature. Everywhere there was for him a Promised Land, in which he recognized the country of his heart. How moving is his use of the word "distances" for the pictures of Poussin and Correggio! It covers a whole philosophy or a whole experience. Common souls content themselves with *foregrounds*, which can be touched. For the sensitive soul, happiness lies beyond; in a perpetual distance, its details are "half hidden by the air." Poussin's great landscapes have the majesty of nature; like her, they are "tender and sublime"; they encompass you, they envelop you. Inaccessible and impenetrable at the time, later they take on a "celestial hue" in our thoughts. In *La Chartreuse*, Stendhal says of Fabrice, as he contemplates Lake Como, "He was only spasmodically vain, and the mere aspect of sublime beauty brought a lump to his throat and took away the bitter and hard edge from his sorrows." Clearly this describes Stendhal himself. He had often blunted the bitter and hard edge of his unhappy love affairs by looking at pictures. A "sublime" nature immersed him in the same joy, the same tender melancholy, as a work of art.

To neglect the foregrounds, to consider only the distances,

the seat of tender and sublime happiness—what a spiritualistic conception for an outrageous materialist!

Stendhal often made mistakes, in art as in love, because nothing ever deceived him and he never lied to himself. He listened only to his heart. This, which governed all his actions, attracted him to women who were incapable of loving him and to works by artists less great than he. In all sincerity, he loved and admired far below his own level. What he says of the insipid Correggio makes the same rending sound as what he says, in a hundred different places, of the dry Métilde or the wanton Angela (even so, the latter offered him a few good moments—see the *Journal* of 1814 and 1815). One is astonished at seeing his great soul overwhelmed by objects so unworthy of it; but this lack of perspicacity, this kind of modesty, even humility, this blind submission to what brought him happiness, also compels admiration. It reveals a stern logic of the emotions and a complete lack of vanity, in relation not only to the world but also to himself. One could never imagine Stendhal thinking, "Such a woman is unworthy of me" (a comic phrase), or "Such a work is unworthy of my admiration," as soon as he had read a promise of happiness on the face of either. Werther never asked himself whether Charlotte was worthy of his love: he thought only of the happiness her existence gave him. So it was with Stendhal. Happiness is the universal yardstick for a man of sensibility, the natural enemy of vulgarity. He never thought himself *above* the world, but on a level with it. He had a passion for equality, and he began with himself. He found this equality in his heart. The idea of putting a bullet through his head for a whore like Signora Pietragrua didn't strike him as in any way ridiculous (*Journal*, October 16, 1814). To have as little vanity before works of art as before women is an almost unique lesson in anti-snobbism and simplicity. Nothing could be less French.

Conversely, when his heart was not drawn to something whose beauty was beyond dispute, he did not restrain himself. Rubens, a far greater artist than Correggio, provoked in him no spurious admiration, no pose. "Rubens, owing to the repulsiveness of his women's bosoms and knees . . . never gave me much pleasure," he ingenuously writes in his *Journal* (1811). Even with the most sensitive souls, in art as in love, the greatest beauty does not always give the greatest joy. One simply has to be sincere with oneself and not blush for one's shortcomings. Beyle's taste for Correggio is a charming weakness (and quite respectable, after all—Correggio is not as bad as Girodet or Delaroche), just as one may choose a woman who is less beautiful, but who promises a happiness more in harmony with one's soul.

Stendhal's predilection for Correggio is not apparent in *L'Histoire de la peinture en Italie*, where he writes delightfully about Giotto, Ghirlandajo, Masaccio and many others, and where he devotes two whole books to Michelangelo and Leonardo. Michelangelo was certainly a character after his own heart. He was Branciforte.

40 *He never paid much attention to architecture and regarded monuments only from the viewpoint of their picturesqueness, without caring whether they were suited to their purpose. He had a horror of everything that was ugly and depressing, and he found these two defects in our national architecture. I think I taught him to distinguish between a Romanesque and a Gothic church and, what is more, how to look at both of them; but he enveloped them both in the same anathema. "Our gloomy and lugubrious churches were invented," he used to say, "by rascally monks who hoped to get rich by putting fear into the timid." Italian Renaissance architecture pleased him on account of its elegance and stylishness. Moreover, he cared only for its graceful details, not at all for its general dispositions. In spite of Lo-gic, this judgment was the fruit not of reason but of his imagination.*

THERE ARE certain expressions for which one has a special affection. I don't know why, but I have always been fond of "The scales fell from his eyes." This doesn't apply to Stendhal, for the simple reason that he possessed the most piercing eyes in the world, without the trace of a scale upon them. "The incredulous man, a rare being," says Alain at the start of his masterly study of him. "Incredulous" must here be understood in the sense of one who never believes what he is told but trusts only his intuition. But this beginning is rather obscure as far as the above passage from Mérimée is concerned. The following may shed a little light.

One of the charms of reading Stendhal is that one never finds what one expects. Take his *Mémoires d'un Touriste*; one finds a certain picturesqueness inherent in the romantic period: journeys by stagecoach, inns, encounters, now vanished crafts and, finally, an aspect of French provincial life which coincides with Balzac's descriptions. But there is above all a way of seeing things that is Stendhal's alone. He looked at France, which was his native land, where he had lived since birth, through the eyes of an Iroquois or a Huron and, what is still more remarkable, *without doing this on purpose.*

I read *Les Mémoires d'un Touriste* when I was about eighteen. My mind was still full of the accepted ideas with which the young are saturated in every country in the world. I was continuously astonished. The truth about dozens of little things appeared naked before me. As I was honest, I was not shocked but amazed. *The scales fell from my eyes.* Here at last was a man in complete disagreement with everything my teachers and family had told me, who confirmed what my instinct dared not assert out loud.

Stendhal found many French landscapes poor and ugly. I remember the feelings with which I reacted to this opinion at the time. I had traveled much through France by car. Before the dreary plains of Beauce, before the most desolate regions in the departments of the north, even before certain sinister villages of the Loire, the grownups around me kept repeating that France was the most beautiful country in the world. This had to be true, since so many respectable people said so and one read it in the papers. It was nature that was in the wrong, or I, who didn't know how to see. Stendhal set me free on this score, as on so many other, more important things.

I took a dislike to the churches and cathedrals of France between ten and fifteen, from hearing their sublimity extolled by people who were incapable of appreciating the slightest real beauty and who had taught me, by their repeated stupidities, never to believe any of their remarks. Patently, they admired only the cathedrals of Reims or Amiens because they were classified monuments, labeled wonders, and because it was the thing to praise them to the skies. Children are never deceived; having themselves a great experience of telling lies, they detect them with remarkable ease. Lo-gic also played its part: How could people who lived in hideous apartments, recommended me nothing but inept books to read and condemned everything I admired, fail to be wrong as well about cathedrals?

I myself saw the churches I was forced to visit as they were, and even a bit more dismal. The image of piety in France seemed to me profoundly sad. It gave me depressing thoughts of chastisement, it evoked an austere Paradise almost worse than hell. Romanesque and Gothic alike bored me, because of their primitive sculptures, in which I saw nothing but crudeness, distortion or clumsiness. To this, perhaps, I owe the aversion I have always felt for primitive art. Only polished, skilled, classical art, nurtured on centuries of experience, moves me. Add to all this one aspect of religion which Stendhal didn't know: the "modern" ignominies manufactured at St.-Sulpice since Napoleon III, to which priests are so addicted and with which they cram their hapless churches. In my childhood, religion had in many places already assumed the vulgar and shabby features of suburban villas. I had known niggardly, cheerless and rascally priests; everything in these places of worship brought them back to me and, I must say in all honesty, filled me with horror.

As with Stendhal, the revelation of religous architecture came to me in Italy, where the cathedrals are like opera houses. I compared the cathedral at Pisa, so gay, so graceful and at the same time grandiose, with the sinister basilicas erected in

France in the thirteenth century. The more the Middle Ages disheartened and oppressed me, the more I delighted in the Renaissance. In St. Peter's in Rome I saw a sort of ecclesiastical Versailles. Religion in Italy seemed to me to have set up a despotism of happiness very different from the morose tyranny of French religion, and I began to love it. In all this one can measure the part played by the spirit of contradiction.

For a child with a religious upbringing in France, everything from the age of five revolves around his parish church, everything converges on it. If the child is not particularly inspired with any religious feeling, the church seems a very sinister place, where he is bored and where he is forbidden to make any noise under pain of offending the Lord and going to hell, a place ruled over by cross-grained old spinsters who smell nasty; where he has to spend hours on end (and an hour is an eternity at the age of ten) because of the service, which is always the same, and the sermon, which is always stupid. Such was the church I knew between 1925 and 1935, in Paris and the provinces. I had no faith, so I was mightily bored, with a lurking fear that my boredom was sacrilegious. Toward fifteen or sixteen, I was struck by the frivolity of the congregation, who went to Mass as if to a bad play—to be seen. "These people are hypocrites," I thought, "who are just performing a social rite. Ugh!" Finally, owing to mischance I met only stupid priests who crudely made propaganda as crude as that of the political parties.

It is difficult to love or admire what has bored or frightened one all one's childhood. The formalist, mundane, hollow, futile Church of my time alienated me from God. I had to forget it, rid my world of it entirely, prevent it from intervening, before I could return to Him, before what little faith my heart contained and which it had nearly obliterated could revive, blossom and take possession of my thoughts. Even now I cannot enter a church without being filled with melancholy. Those countless hours of boredom during my childhood rise up in my throat and irremediably color all religious architecture for me. The Cathedral of Chartres, although so beautiful, will never give me the same pleasure as the Château de Chambord. As I have said, I came to like churches only when I discovered those of Italy, which spoke to me of another God, of a joyful and delightful God. The priests of Italy are more rascally than those of France, and they put more fear into the timid, of whom there is besides a far greater number in Italy than at home; even so, they haven't frightened *me*. No doubt because I was nearly thirty when I first met them.

One shudders to think what religion was like in Grenoble at the end of the *ancien régime:* just as narrow but much more powerful than in 1925. The Church, for Stendhal, was indissolubly bound up with his unhappy childhood, and he loathed it with a constancy that I haven't shown. I am convinced that his aversion for religious architecture springs from that; it reminded him too much of his miseries as a child. One can dispute Stendhal's tastes, but not his strength of character. In this matter he gives proof of the same lack of pose as in everything else. The heart of this incredulous man is a *tabula rasa:* he allows into it only what he likes. Impossible to sway him. He uses his own truth as a universal touchstone.

Stendhal had no dearer wish than to quit Grenoble. He achieved this thanks to mathematics. At sixteen he was sent to Paris. The ugliness of the suburbs filled him with depression. This depression became despair when he discovered that Paris was not surrounded by mountains like Grenoble. At that time he was a poet, something like "a hundredth part of Tasso." Abruptly parted from the beautiful landscapes of the Dauphiné and precipitated into mud, he lapsed into a sort of listlessness. Shortly after, employed by his relative Pierre Daru, he consoled himself with a few lime trees planted in the ministry garden, behind which the clerks went to relieve themselves. In the spring, "the limes put out buds, finally they had leaves; I was deeply moved; at last I had friends in Paris!" he writes in *Brulard*.

Stendhal loved nature bare and unadorned. His heroes dream before wild or romantic landscapes; he himself, in the country, was filled with daydreams or brimming over with happiness. Before trees, rivers, the sea, man "feels the gravity of his position and the value of life," says Alain, adding, "It is then that we bestride time; it is then that we long to catch up with unfeeling nature and race with her. And this is exactly the effect of music." Nature bare and unadorned does not deceive us; it goes straight to the depths of our hearts, to seek out the sorrows that gnaw at us. Artists and men of sensibility feel this deeply around the age of fifteen. If they are then removed into a town, their need of beauty throws them back on architecture. I forget where Stendhal reveals how suddenly, one fine day, he began to understand it. This was in the Paris of 1799, just after the close of the *ancien régime*, therefore still very beautiful, very noble, even rather pathetic, like Marie Antoinette in the Temple. In Paris nature no longer obscured architecture for him, and his artist's soul was waiting only for this, for this "natural" curtain to be drawn, to greet in her this first (or new) art.

In the first lines of his paragraph, Mérimée unwittingly defines the difference between his own conception of architecture and that of his friend. He speaks like an inspector of monuments, like a friend of Viollet-le-Duc (a much-maligned man who saved many things), like one of the profession, if I may put it that way. He speaks as an architect. Compared with him, Stendhal was an amateur, a dilettante, an aesthete, who enjoyed a building in the same way as a picture or a piece of music, "without caring whether it was suited to its purpose." The pleasure of art was enough for him; he cared not a fig, so to speak, for the story behind it. A wise and modest attitude, at the opposite pole from that of the ordinary tourist, who *visits* everything he comes across and has it *explained* to him.

Architecture is the introduction and the mark of man in the midst of nature, the addition of a new beauty to an immemorial one. But nature, at least in Europe, is never unadorned. Men have modeled, redesigned, shaped her to their use. Even when she is empty and without buildings, man is everywhere present, be it only in his network of roads, which is always beautiful, as Alain says, because it embraces the contours of the earth. The house or monument in the middle of a landscape is merely the final touch given by man to this nature he has planned. The monument crowns the landscape, makes it sing. This, to my mind, is one of the ways that can lead a man of sensibility to the pleasures of architecture. But this way, unfortunately, Mérimée can hardly be said to have taken.

41

Beyle had been an officer for some months and, as an auditor, had followed several campaigns, including the Russian one in 1812, with the Emperor's headquarters. We loved to hear him talk of the campaigns he had been on with Napoleon. His stories bore absolutely no resemblance to the official accounts, as will be seen. Naturally brave, he had observed the war coldly and with curiosity. Without being indifferent to the great and poetic scenes he had witnessed, he above all enjoyed describing its more bizarre and grotesque aspects. Besides, he had a horror of the exaggerations of national vainglory and, out of a spirit of contradiction, often went too far in the opposite direction. Like Courier, he made merciless fun of what has since been called chauvinism, *an emotion which after all has its good side, since it makes a conscript fight like a veteran soldier.*

WITHOUT wishing to annoy anyone, I have to admit that I don't hear with quite the same feelings a naturally brave man and a coward making fun of chauvinism. I approve of the former, I allow him every right to his mockery, for in his case it is gratuitous, it offers proof of his freedom of mind, of his just assessment of human vanity; it is, moreover, a sign of modesty, for it is elegant to make so light of something for which one is so gifted. The spirit of contradiction, on the other hand, sets me against the latter. I see how much it is in the coward's interest to make fun of chauvinism, and that spoils the mockery for me, however subtle and even justified it may be.

The coward's position is a delicate one. There are certain burning topics on which he should forbid himself to enlarge. Military valor, for instance, or chauvinism; for, whatever he says, he is suspect. If he praises chauvinism, he is the worst kind of hypocrite (the sort that flourished luxuriantly between 1871 and 1914); if he lashes out at it, his protests are due to fear. We have a host of examples today of this second type of coward. They lord it in the "progressive" newspapers and uphold the theory that one isn't a thorough intellectual unless one is afraid of violence.*

With us, defeatism thrives on a flattering ambiguity. France having been a brave, warlike, very united and usually victorious nation, to be defeatist was a manifestation of courage until about 1935. The defeatists were for a long time genuine nonconformists and were persecuted—a difficult and perilous position, of course, but one which engendered real gratifications of conscience. The defeatist opposes natural morality to social morality and feels invincible. He is. His security is absolute. If social morality is firmly established and harsh, he represents the indomitable right of the individual, all-powerful by reason of its weakness, before the oppressor. He is the only just man before the wicked.

Nations go through unhappy periods of weakness or despondency, when natural morality replaces social morality in public opinion. But natural morality does not suit a nation. It leads inevitably to slavery or savagery, which are two appalling evils. One couldn't have done better than give lessons in natural morality to the France of 1810 or 1910, even to the

---

* It must under no circumstances be thought that this attitude is the prerogative of the leftists. We have seen the right wing, jingoistic until 1939, turn suddenly defeatist in 1940, under the pressure of we know what events. These are the normal variations of conformity.

France of Louis Philippe and Doumergue. France was then arrogant, unscrupulous, still very powerful in spite of setbacks, and almost blindly faithful to social morality. None of this deceived Stendhal; or, rather, his spirit of contradiction was not deceived. He told himself, moreover, that so great a country had no need of his small voice to defend it. The official thinkers saw to that, and the unanimous concert of adulation for the country stirred his heart. He should have known the France of 1955! No one then had the slightest interest in his country any longer, save for a few out-of-date provincials, who hardly dared admit that they loved their country and were prepared to die for it, so heartily would everyone have laughed at them. I am quite sure that Stendhal's spirit of contradiction would have brought him down on the side of those poor suffering souls and that he too would have adopted the ridiculous attitude of a patriot, just as he was an ardent "patriot" between 1799 and 1804, so much devotion, disinterest, enthusiasm and passion did he see among the soldiers and officials of the Republic. The curse of patriotism is that its language is always the same, and most people heed nothing but the language. In 1955, it used the same words as in 1914, but their content was different. In 1914 it was quite simple to be a patriot. In 1955 it was the hardest thing in the world. So at the time it was the sole attitude that a proud man had the right to choose.

I want to make it clear that I am in no way trying to travesty history. I am in no way trying to turn Stendhal into a wild patriot, a Barrès or a Henry Bordeaux. I merely note that men's characters react according to the circumstances, and that it is not impossible that such a contradictory spirit as Stendhal, who cared only for unfrequented places, who was either so severe or so indifferent toward the intolerant and quarrelsome France he knew, would have revealed a similarly refractory nature toward a weak France, indifferent to her fate, disowning herself, wallowing in abasement and setting up as her prophets the very men who were exhorting her to die. Mérimée's sentence is revealing: ". . . he had a horror of the exaggerations of national vainglory and, out of a spirit of contradiction, often went too far in the opposite direction." One is tempted to recast this sentence inversely, so that it would reflect a Stendhalian spirit in 1955: "He had a horror of the exaggerations of national defeatism and, out of a spirit of contradiction, often went too far in the opposite direction."

To describe war in its more bizarre and grotesque aspects is a temptation it would be hard to resist when one was living in an epic age, when everything resounded with cries of victory, when the country was intoxicated by superhuman deeds, exaggerated still further by *Le Moniteur* and repeated in bombastic tones by the official publicists, historians and propagandists. Not to mention a love of truth, of its comic side and it syncopations, that real artistic pleasure that the naked, unvarnished truth gives, and finally the joy (superior to any other for an artist) of "catching a likeness." Here is a passage from *Brulard,* written twenty-five years after, which has the complete ring of truth. It is by a reliable man who lies neither to himself nor to others:

> . . . when, in 1811, I was an auditor and, two weeks later, a surveyor of the imperial household, I was drunk for three months with contentment at no longer being a paymaster exposed to the envy and malice of those gross heroes who were the Emperor's laborers at Jena and Wagram. Posterity will never know the coarseness and stupidity of those men when off the battlefield. And even on the battlefield, what prudence! They were like Admiral Nelson, the hero of Naples, always thinking of what each wound would bring them by way of gratuities and medals. What ignoble beasts, compared with the high

virtues of General Michaud or Colonel Mathis. No, posterity will never know what downright oafs those heroes of Napoleon's bulletins were, and how I used to laugh when I received *Le Moniteur* in Vienna, Dresden, Berlin or Moscow—which almost no one in the army received, in order to prevent any derision over the lies. The "bulletins" were weapons of war, part of the campaign, and not pieces of history.

Let us put as a pendant to this admirably frank description (which cost him nothing, for nothing for him was simpler than naïvely to tell the truth) the "great and poetic" military scenes at the beginning of *La Chartreuse* and the pages in *La Vie de Napoléon* referring to the campaign in Italy. I might add that the fact of depicting warriors as they are, namely, "sword holders," doesn't prevent one from feeling a veteran amidst a craven society which disowns them. The "sword holders" are what they are; for all that one may assess them at their true worth, one prefers them even so to what comes after them.

I would like the reader to turn back to page 34, where we see Beyle clutching one boot in the middle of a rout. It is the portrait of a man who rises above circumstances, who shows bravery in a place where everyone is afraid. He is a soldier of the Revolution amidst soldiers of the Empire, just as he was to be a Bonapartist under the Restoration. Guelf for the Ghibellines, Ghibelline for the Guelfs, such was the way of this man in love with solitude. Stendhal always rose above circumstances, for he judged them and, having judged them, did not bow to them, never let himself be led by them. In judging "the Emperor's manual laborers" coldly and for what they were, by recording their strength and weakness as he did with every man he met, by never being blinded or hidebound, he was never taken in by life. In other words, he displayed his enthusiasm only when there was good cause, not at random. He didn't content himself with externals, which are always splendid or striking, grandiose or tragic, and at which most men stop. He wanted to know the motives, the hidden reasons —in fact, the soul, to speak his own language.

What makes one realize that with Stendhal one is dealing with a truly superior, even unique, man, and not with a commonplace misanthropist or a crude pessimist, is the fact that he recognized just as clearly and casually nobility and baseness, virtue and vice, courage and cowardice, cupidity and disinterest, the sublime and the abject. Everything was equal in his eyes. Which didn't prevent him from being an ardent moralist, from tirelessly condemning vice and being infinitely moved by virtue.

For Stendhal war was an adventure like any other, with its ups and downs and different generations of men. The soldiers of the Republic were hardly at all like those of the Empire. The former—young, gay, happy, unshod, indifferent to promotion, solely concerned with liberty and the joy of fighting for it, in love with Lombardy and the beautiful blondes of Milan—filled him with a positively passionate feeling of friendship. He found them all delightful. In the Sixth Dragoons in 1801 he felt at home, with his true family. These were not the same soldiers of whom the Emperor could say to Berthier, "I have an income of a hundred thousand men." The soldiers of the Revolution were not "laborers" but free men, inflamed by ideas, not by medals. If they formed an income at all, it was for their country. The soldiers of 1809 and 1812 were heroes, no doubt, but also egoists, with the exception of the "amiable Lasalle," of Moncey, "who wouldn't have stooped to certain things," and of the "great Gouvion-Saint-Cyr." One can guess, a hundred and fifty years later, how bored Stendhal was by the Grande Armée. There must have been no member of it with whom he could exchange the simplest idea. I too have a slight knowledge of the army. Not a conquering army, alas, or drunk with victory, but a French army organized like Napoleon's and one which, for a brief moment, could hold its head high. In it I never came across a single noble thought. Nothing but shabby schemes for getting invalided out, or procuring a rank, or profiteering. I suppose all armies are like that, including the Grande Armée. One accommodates oneself just as comfortably to glory and epic deeds as to defeat and abasement. Whatever one does, "life goes on," that is to say the little emotions, the cheap revenges, the unworthy desires, the rancors, the self-interest. The lapse of time obliterates these petty details, and only the grandeur remains. But it is another thing to have lived through it all. I can understand how Stendhal, exasperated by the ceaseless bragging of the officers retired on half pay and the legend so skillfully fostered by Louis Philippe, was led out of pure reaction to describe the bizarre or grotesque aspects of an adventure which he knew as well as most men. Better, even, for he had seen it through the eyes of a lynx.

In highly passionate men, provided that they are intelligent, have some idea of the relativity of the human being to the universe and know, finally, that beyond a certain point one can have no further influence on events, there is a basic indifference, a germ of renunciation. Once they realize that they can do no more, they instantly transform themselves into spectators. The spirit of action gives way to that of observation and criticism. In the middle of the Grande Armée and the victories of the French armies, Stendhal had a hundred occasions to realize his insignificance and feel his inability to influence the prodigious events that surrounded him on every side. From these, the moments he selected to sit back in his heart as if it were a seat in a theater and watch the play with complete detachment, came his observation of its "bizarre and grotesque aspects."

When Stendhal speaks of Napoleon, he compares him quite naturally to Alexander the Great. After the retreat from Russia, it doubtless became clear to his piercing eye that destiny had gained the upper hand (though not without his having shed light on the human reasons for this defeat) and that there was nothing more to be done.

He stoutly denied all the harangues, all the sublime words spoken on the battle-fields. "Do you know what military elo-quence is?" he used to ask us. "Here is an example: In a very hot affray, one of our bravest cavalry generals harangued his troops, who were close to breaking rank, in these terms: 'For-ward, you swine! My arse is as round as an apple! My arse is as round as an apple!' The comic thing about it is that, in this moment of danger, it seemed so like any other harangue that they wheeled about and repulsed the enemy. You may be sure that Caesar and Alexander, on similar occasions, addressed their soldiers in no less sublime a fashion."

THE VETERANS I have known can be drawn up in two cate-gories: the boasters and the realists. The stories of the former exaggerated the facts and embellished them, giving their ad-ventures a gay or epic twist. Those of the latter, on the other hand, showed war in all its squalor and suffering. These two tendencies are to be found in the countless novels that the war inspired between 1915 and 1930. They are similarly to be found in the war memorials scattered throughout France which represent poilus sometimes ferociously brandishing their rifles, sometimes expiring in the arms of a veiled and weeping woman. One ought to take a census of these monu-ments, bearing in mind that the expiring poilu implies a left-wing municipality, and the ferocious poilu a more or less right-wing one. This would provide a good political map of France in about 1922.

To have been in the army is always a privilege; at least it leaves an experience. However antimilitarist one may be, one feels a faint superiority over those who have never been soldiers. One knows something they don't, which for them is a huge mystery. What is the army? What does the army think? What does it want? What is the "brotherhood of arms," that emotion which must exist, as it has been so often referred to ever since the world began? Stendhal, a veteran, knew all about it. He had an intimate knowledge of that "different" spirit which men assume together with their uniforms, of the erosion caused by regimental life and battle on men's souls. He knew the ways, language and peculiarities of soldiers.

But he doesn't describe everything at random, like a simpleton who can't get over what he has seen. The "great and poetic scenes" are taken for granted. Don't count on him either to bewail the horrors of war, which equally go without saying. This man of truth was as far from the aggressive as from the martyr poilu. He was interested only in the true poilu, an animal as fascinating to study as a hedgehog or a tortoise, who has to be seen in his true aspect, in his true character, with his virtues and his vices, his comic and tragic sides. I hasten to add that I have almost never heard a veteran talk like Stendhal. And yet men at war, whether suffering or victorious, are still men. There is no more reason to lie about them than there is to lie about man in general. But how is one to make this simple observation comprehensible to people who live in the permanent falsehood of morals, progaganda, self-interest and education, that is to say almost the whole population of the globe?

The army is an immense club, a freemasonry, whose members recognize each other at a glance. Between two men who have waged war, were they at opposite poles as regards their characters, ideas or upbringing, there exists an understanding, a familiarity, which they do not find with people closer to them. Stendhal and Mérimée, so close on so many fields, did not understand each other on this one. Mérimée knew nothing of the army nor of war, and I feel that he didn't entirely grasp the anecdote he quotes. I myself have long brooded over it, and a few little things have occurred to me, which I give here.

The general in question was Murat. Let us try to imagine what the relations between officers and men were like under the Empire. Despite the discipline and the hordes of counts and dukes created by the Emperor, there still remained a good deal of Revolutionary bonhomie. It must also be remembered that this Napoleonic army included about a hundred stars, generals or marshals laden with victories, famous for definite reasons that had been weighed by connoisseurs (that is, by the whole army), not only sanctioned by the Emperor but also "ratified" by the men themselves. I wasn't there, of course, but I can guess that the rank and file prided themselves on some slight familiarity with these heroes, shouted to them as they passed, the way one does to old friends who have had more brilliant careers than one's own, or like the stagehands in a theater when they pass the leading man. It's a matter of impressing one's pals, of showing that one is somebody by being on familiar terms with the boss.

Murat, prince and king though he was, had certainly kept the bluff and hearty ways of "one of the boys." He must have been the "soldier's friend," gay, simple and not a bit arrogant. No doubt he went in the evenings to joke with the corporals and veterans round the campfire. This was part of his style, just as it was to get himself up in fancy dress with gold braid up to his eyes and plumes two feet high. Add that the men had seen him in action more than once, and that he was so fine a soldier that the Emperor had taken him for his brother-in-law. Haughty generals are the ones who do no fighting. Those who pay with their persons, who give as good as the next man with their sabers, who don't believe they were born from Jupiter's thigh, inspire ardent friendship and respect among their men. This results in a display of familiarity which is the subtlest and highest form of discipline. Murat was incomparable in a cavalry charge; he led them like a whirlwind. Superb, into the bargain, and quite devoid of braggadocio. All this was quite enough to send every squadron mad for love of him.

Now to examine the anecdote. Firstly, one learns that the cavalry was about to break rank. One is struck by the absurdity of what Murat shouts: "My arse is as round as an apple! My arse is as round as an apple!" Indeed, I cannot help feeling here that Stendhal omitted the key to his story. This wasn't just "like any other harangue." It is much too ludicrous to have no meaning, as Mérimée thought. It has, on the contrary, a very precise one.

According to the context, the cavalry were in a bad way. They had already charged once or twice without result, save to lose men. Was the bugler no longer at his post? A cavalry charge must make a fearsome noise; the horses thunder over the ground, the cuirassiers clank like saucepans, everyone yells like a redskin: on top of all this, the bugler blows fit to burst, sounding the charge as loud as he can, blowing the fiercest notes he can. It is he who gives rhythm to the gallop and turns it into something really formidable, beautiful in its way, like the finale of the Emperor Concerto, something which flays the nerves and inflames the men's hearts with hatred for the enemy.

In the heat of battle, soldiers become cannibals, the conquering captains are as savage as tribal kings. An incoherent yell, a meaningless leap, a grimace, anything serves to revive their ardor if ever it shows signs of flagging. But that wasn't the case here. I think (I am even almost sure) that what Murat shouted, or sang, if you like, was *the charge*—no more and no less. Everyone knows how soldiers love to put bawdy or comic words to military bugle calls. Well, "My arse is as round as an apple!" was precisely that. Although it has been impossible for me to verify, I would stake my life that these were the comic words the cuirassiers or dragoons of 1806 had concocted to fit the bugle call of the charge.

The bugler is dead. Who is to replace him? Murat, with his stentorian voice. Perhaps he couldn't sing in tune. So that there should be no mistake, so that they should all know they were embarking on a new charge, he yelled the familiar words more or less to the required rhythm. At the head of his squadrons, galloping like a madman, he sang the charge, he took the bugler's place, he became a one-man band. This, I believe, is the hidden meaning of Stendhal's little story. To me, it is as fine as Leonidas at Thermopylae. It maddens me that Mérimée should have failed to understand it. He was the sort of man who would have adored it.

Another example of martial eloquence: "After leaving Moscow, we got lost on the third day of the retreat and, as night fell, found ourselves, numbering about 1,500 men, separated from the main body by a strong Russian division. We spent part of the night bewailing our fate. Then the more forceful harangued the craven with such success that it was determined to open up a way through at swordpoint as soon as daylight permitted us to distinguish the enemy. You needn't suppose they said, 'Brave soldiers,' and so on. No. 'You scum, you'll all be dead tomorrow, since you're too f—— scared to take up a gun and make use of it.' This heroic address having produced its effect, at the first hint of daybreak we resolutely marched toward the Russians, whose campfires we could still see flickering. We arrived with lowered bayonets without being discovered, to find nothing but a dog all alone. The Russians had left during the night."

I WAS about to say how regrettable it is that we don't have a whole book by Stendhal describing the Napoleonic Wars in this way. But such regrets are absurd. By the same token, it is regrettable that Stendhal did not write about June bugs or the Persians, for he was equipped to write on all subjects, to approach them from original angles and say unique things about them. This is equivalent to regretting that he produced only forty books instead of three thousand.

"Small truths" are the flowers of literature. They illumine

it, giving it life and animation, and make it charming and delightful. In the lesser genre of conversation, they are equally beguiling. No conversation is agreeable without anecdotes or gossip. For gossip, which people pretend to disparage, forms another category of small truth, whose object is to reveal human nature, a moment of human nature. There is scope for a dictionary of small truths taken from Stendhal: small truths on army life, on love, politics, society, the peasantry and so on. This was once attempted, but without plan or sequence, by M. Vaudoyer. I myself have in mind a complete book, a "world of small truths" collected from everywhere, including oral traditions about Beyle. What a wonderful lesson in observation and sensibility this would be for an honest reader!

In the sphere of "small military truths," the one which heads this chapter is a very pretty example. It contains five episodes in a total of seventeen lines, a dramatic progression, two great human attitudes, a natural speech, a moral and a philosophy. Who could say more in fewer words?

The wonderful thing about truth is that it is never humble and that one can always draw a lesson from the slenderest truth, from the smallest detail, provided it is true. This certainly applies here. The adventure of the group of 1,500 men separated from the army by a large Russian division provides in miniature the whole spectacle and philosophy of courage and war. This is as valid for a single man as for a whole nation in arms. The harangue of the forceful is exactly what it should be: pessimistic, insulting, provocative, effective. It does not conceal the truth, which is horrifying; it leaves no way out save boldness. Churchill, in his great speech in June 1940, albeit a little more nobly, said no more to an England on the brink of annihilation and slavery. "Brave soldiers" is demagogy or bombast. "You scum!" is realism and vigor. It is also love, in its way, since its aim is not to please but to save. Words are actions, and one must paint despair if one wants to instill energy. It seems to me that during the war of 1940 we cruelly lacked "forceful" men to say "You scum!" to our armies. Far from this, they tirelessly repeated, "Brave soldiers!" to these voters in uniform. There lies the difference between a victorious and a defeated nation. The historic words pronounced by the defeated are much more beautiful than those of the victorious, for their laziness leaves them plenty of time to polish them. The trouble is that posterity doesn't preserve them.

What was the point, it may be objected, in urging the 1,500 strayed soldiers to bravery, since in any case the Russians had decamped? My reply to that is that one deserves one's good fortune, and with rather shaky logic I would say that it is precisely because the men pulled themselves together that heaven caused their enemies to disappear. The lesson here is that one must always be prepared to face the worst, in order to enjoy the happy surprise of finding nothing. When one is unprepared, the worst will assuredly occur. To say to death "I am not afraid of you" is usually enough to put death to flight.

During the retreat, he said, he did not suffer too much from hunger; but it was absolutely impossible for him to remember how he had eaten or what he had eaten, except for a lump of tallow for which he had paid twenty francs and which he still recalled with intense pleasure.

H OW MANY SOLDIERS' and prisoners' tales have I had to endure! They were never about anything but food. They either gorged themselves or starved. We know by heart the gorgings of the poilus returning from the front in 1914, and the hunger of the prisoners of 1940. What haven't they told us, about sides of beef and oceans of champagne on the one hand, and turnips and dishwater on the other! Of the retreat from Russia, Stendhal could remember only a lump of tallow costing twenty francs. And he still remembered it with intense pleasure. Here is a feature which does him honor and which is scarcely French. I can never have enough praise for the fair-mindedness and moderation of this man, for whom food was just an unimportant detail. What a quality of soul this reveals! He must have been almost unique in his way, and I can well imagine, a hundred and forty years later, the endless tales of famine which the survivors of 1812 brought back from their ordeal. The national character doesn't change so much in a hundred and forty years. Frenchmen must have had just as great appetites then as they have now, and they must have discussed food with similar satisfaction or horror, depending on the circumstances.

It is by such forgetfulness (inability to remember how or what they ate) that one distinguishes noble from vulgar souls. I hardly dare record this banal truth, so great is the power of demagogy today. There will be those who accuse me of insulting misery. Now, I don't find it easy to speak of. I have been poor, and although I didn't experience the retreat from Russia or the concentration camps, I ate very little and very badly between 1941 and 1946, and this left me with a permanently impaired digestion. I apologize for such a naïve and personal detail, but it is things like this that nowadays earn one respect.

45

On leaving Moscow, he had carried with him a copy of Voltaire's Facéties *bound in red morocco, which he had taken from a blazing palace. His comrades reproached him when he read a few pages of it by the light of a campfire in the evening. They found such behavior irresponsible. The idea of breaking up a magnificent edition! He himself felt a kind of remorse, and after a few days he left the book on the snow.*

THIS PARAGRAPH is uncertain both in style and in thought—a very rare thing with Mérimée. The French reads: *"Ses camarades le blâmèrent quand il en lisait . . . ,"* which is a turn of phrase it is hard to justify. The past tense of *"blâmèrent"* expresses a single occasion, whereas the imperfect tense of *"lisait"* implies a repeated action. As for the thought, what behavior did they find irresponsible—reading Voltaire's *Facéties* in such grave circumstances or having broken up the edition? It is interesting to compare this version with the corresponding paragraph in *H.B.* which runs: "He had carried away from Moscow a volume of Voltaire's *Facéties* bound in red morocco, which he had taken from a burning house. His comrades found this action rather irresponsible: the idea of breaking up a magnificent edition! He himself felt a kind of remorse." This second account is shorter but more explicit. Nevertheless, one can see why I preferred, for my exegesis, to use the version from *Portraits historiques et littéraires*, despite its occasional slips. There is more to it. Take the subtlety, for instance, of: "He left the book on the snow." An ordinary writer would have put "in the snow," which would have been flat. "On the snow" is subtle and creates an image. It evokes a furtive, barely deliberate gesture—almost an oversight. Such nuances fascinate me.

To go deeper, we find the following in Stendhal's *Journal* of 1812, where he describes his departure from burning Moscow: "Before leaving the house, I looted from it a volume of Voltaire, the one entitled *Facéties*." Clearly, that was all he looted, a book, when the others were taking china, gold, furniture and so on. There is a small class of soldier for whom, on a campaign, nothing is more precious than a book. When I went off to war in 1940, the first things I put in my knapsack were a volume of Mallarmé and one of Valéry. An odd choice, you may say. But that was my taste at the time. I was just twenty and thought I was in this way taking with me the greatest sum of ideas and beauty in the smallest space. Like pills, so to speak. I mention it only in order to sanction this other, indefensible choice of the *Facéties* made by Stendhal. Perhaps he regarded them as compressed tablets of wit and intellect; perhaps he saw in this collection the best antidote to the cold, hunger and fatigue, to all the vulgarities and horrors that lay ahead of him. Reading these highly civilized fragments in the evening by the light of a campfire, amidst the savagery of men and nature, must have formed a contrast such as he would have appreciated. Anyway, a book weighs nothing, is nothing. I can understand Beyle's thoughts on seeing his fellows laden with sumptuous booty: how looters, by burdening themselves with material goods like this, condemn themselves to the fatigue and worry of transporting them; how they fall into the murderous illusion of possessions, which leads to all kinds of cowardice, dishonor and often death, out of a reluctance to get rid of them. It isn't necessary to be a Christian to loathe covetousness. It is enough to have one's heart in the right place, like Stendhal, and to know that one travels in comfort only if one is naked, especially in the middle of a rout.

One doesn't abdicate one's sensibility and tastes because one makes war. On the contrary, the pleasures of the mind that one contrives to snatch out of all the squalor become singularly acute. Under the date of August 28, 1812, Stendhal notes in his *Journal:*

> *My soul** has been refreshed only *by some music with* Urbs alba [Villeblanche] *made me in* Smolensk; the coldness of this instrument was compensated for by my long privation. I had heard no music since July 22, the eve of my departure for this Russia, to which I in no way regret having come, for here I judge the *War and* what we in our country call heroes calmly: besides, I am acquiring certain rights *to my dear Italy*.

There is another curious passage in the *Journal,* slightly Neronic in spirit, which will make our contemporary lyricists go through the roof and which I cannot resist quoting for their benefit:

> SEPTEMBER 15, 1812.— . . . We left the city lit by the finest conflagration in the world, forming a pyramid which was like the prayers of the faithful, the base being on the ground and the point in heaven. The moon appeared, I think, above the flames. It was a wonderful sight, but one really should have been alone to see it, or else surrounded by kindred spirits. This is the sad circumstance which has spoiled the campaign in Russia for me—the fact that I have made it with people who would belittle the Colosseum or the Bay of Naples.

---

* The words italicized in this extract are the same English words that Stendhal himself used.

Could anyone be less demagogic? Show me a writer today who would dare to write something as insolent, simply because it was true.

To have done with the burning of Moscow, here is a last extract from the *Journal*, revealing a perfect sagacity and freedom of mind: "We could clearly see the vast pyramid made by the pianos and settees of Moscow, which would have given us such joy were it not for the mania to burn. This Rostopchin* will be a scoundrel or a Roman; one must wait and see how his affair progresses." The whole of Stendhal is in this passage, and every word of it is a delight.

---

* The Russian governor of Moscow.—Tr.

He was one of the few who, in the midst of all the miseries our army had to endure in the disastrous retreat from Moscow, always preserved their moral strength, the respect of others and of themselves. One day, in the vicinity of the Berezina, Beyle reported to his chief, M. Daru, shaved and dressed with considerable care. "So you've removed your beard, monsieur?" said M. Daru. "You have a stout heart."

*R*odrigue, as-tu du coeur?" Grammar-school teachers, when making their pupils consider this famous question, say that "heart" here means courage. I myself see in it a finer and wider meaning. "Heart" is not only courage; it also encompasses a desire to try one's strength, a nobility of character, a horror of what is base or vulgar, *espagnolisme*, a passion for honor—in short, soul. And soul precisely as Alain defines it. Heart is what refuses the body. What, for instance, refuses to flee when the body trembles, what refuses to strike when the body is provoked, what refuses to remain hairy and dirty when the body is ravaged by cold and want during the retreat from Russia. The madman has no strength to refuse; he has no more *heart*. In 1812, at the Berezina, all the men were mad with pain and desperation. They had no heart left, save for a few, including Stendhal (and General Eblé's pontoniers).

"A stout heart," said M. Daru. I can imagine that Stendhal felt honored all his life by such a tribute and always recalled it with pleasure. To shave near the Berezina is an act comparable to that of the thirsty Alexander the Great pouring the water out of his helmet. How rare to find a man one can admire without reserve, in every part of his life, whose actions never belie his thoughts or doctrines, but even tend to enhance them. With writers, the opposite is so much more often the case! How many cowards there are for one Socrates who dies a hero, and how often our intellectual masters give us opportunities to despise them in their lives! One sees every day that it is easier to have intellect, wit and philosophy than heart, or, if you prefer it, soul. Wars have at least this much good, that they permit us to see the souls of those we admire. Danger brings out the soul as rain brings out snails.

I can clearly picture Stendhal being asked in each grave circumstance of his life by some great figure out of Corneille: "Henri, have you heart?" This modest man, this friend of understatement, refrains from replying in Alexandrines; he just gives a knowing smile or a faintly facetious wink. To have heart is the least of things; that goes without saying. Stendhal gives his hand to the Cid, to old Horace, to Polyeucte, to Nicomedes; but during the intervals of the adventure, during the dead times of *espagnolisme*, he takes them to spend an hour at the brothel.

To yield to circumstances is humiliating. The spirit of contradiction cannot endure it. But I suddenly realize, after all these pages, that the spirit of contradiction is quite simply soul, in Alain's sense of the word, or heart, as understood by Don Diègue* and M. Daru. It is no use disdainfully sighing, "Words, words, words!" Words are very useful for opening up ideas, for helping one idea to link up with another, for advancing further, for discovering oneself. People without heart, that is to say people who display no spirit of contradiction in adversity, are tedious. I have had experience of them

* In Corneille's famous *Le Cid.*—Tr.

several times. In 1940, in a prisoner-of-war camp, and in 1944, sharing a cell with nine or ten political prisoners condemned to death, I had ample time to study the two categories of individuals who people the world: the first, very limited in number, composed of men with stout hearts, gay, loquacious and intrepid, taking their hardships lightly, tirelessly thinking up plans for resistance or escape, "making a virtue of necessity"; and the second, very numerous, composed of dispirited men, exaggerating their woes, morose, taciturn, sick at heart, ceaselessly trembling for their miserable skins, deprived by fear of all spirit, incapable of thinking of anything but the calamities that await them and therefore horribly passive and devoid of conversation. As cowards are the most numerous, it is they, alas, who form public opinion, and they call the men of heart unfeeling in order to justify or gild their misery.

To shave and make oneself spick and span in the middle of the retreat from Russia in order to report to one's hierarchical superior means this: "What I consider suitable in Paris, what is *done*, holds good for anywhere else, regardless of temperature, inconvenience or military defeat. To give in, in the face of stupidities like the rout of an army of half a million men, famine and so on, is unworthy of a gallant man who hasn't lost his razor and who knows how to sew on buttons. It is vital not to let oneself go, for then one finds oneself in a flash at the bottom of hell."

I put all this into words, but it is actually done almost without thinking. The spirit of contradiction (or heart) dispenses with reasoning. It reacts almost automatically and goes straight to the most difficult point, which, for it, is the easiest. Of two ills, wallowing in the general vulgarity or performing feats of valor to avoid renouncing any of one's aristocratic habits, it chooses the lesser, which is the second one. This second ill is not an ill, moreover, since it implies activity, and as soon as one ceases to be passive one ceases to be unhappy.

Whenever I chance from time to time to meet one of my comrades in captivity, military or political, I am always delighted. I am reminded that during the brief period I spent in the camp or in prison I passed the time telling funny stories or organizing practical jokes, and that my good humor, which almost never failed me, was sometimes precious to them. Every man has his claims to glory. This is almost the only one that matters to me, and I hope I shall be excused for my touch of vanity in reporting it. In my bad moments, I tell myself that I too have in my time been "stouthearted." Besides, through a paradox of character, danger makes me merry, and all the more so when it exasperates the prudent who share it with me. I shall arouse the indignation of the superstitious pacifists of our time when I say that I do not hate war. One doesn't hate what makes one happy. In the face of danger, I clearly see my soul leave my body and reign alone. How can one despise such moments? I certainly subscribe to everything against war: it is horrible, monstrous, ignoble. But it has given me joys that I have found nowhere else. The few people to whom I have confided this have indulgently replied, "What you are saying was true for war in the old days; it no longer applies today, with flame throwers and ten-ton bombs." Yet I never fought in the wars of the old days.

I shall stop here, for fear of repeating what has already been expressed by better writers, Vigny among them. I apologize once again for the presumption of this chapter, but I must confess I felt it worth while to do a little boasting about bravery. This offsets the boasting about cowardice which has flourished for the past twenty years.

M. Bergonié, auditor to the Privy Council and attached to headquarters, told me that he owed his life to Beyle, who, foreseeing the congestion on the bridges over the Berezina, made him cross to the opposite bank on the evening preceding the rout. He almost had to use force to persuade M. Bergonié to walk those few hundred paces. M. Bergonié had the highest praise for Beyle's coolness and good sense, which never deserted him at a time when the most resolute were losing their heads. Beyle was a man of resource in grave circumstances; he used to say modestly that he owed this advantage to his store of ready-made maxims, by means of which he found himself ready to act when others were wasting time wondering what to do.

Coolness and good sense are the two prizes which destiny grants to people who feel gay and lighthearted in the face of danger. "Honor is quite simply the highest form of good sense," said Bernanos. Fear heats, it creates steam and clouds the brain. When one is gay and lighthearted, one has a clear mind, one calculates accurately, one *foresees*. The episode of the taxis of the Marne in September 1914 is a good example. Gallieni was a man whom the war made gay and lighthearted. The taxis of the Marne was a Stendhalian idea, that is to say the idea of a man of maxims, who reduces complex problems to known theorems. Under the circumstances, and to repeat one of Stendhal's formulas relative to Napoleon, "Get your troops onto the battlefield by no matter what means, so as always to have two soldiers against one soldier of the enemy." The philosophy of the taxis of the Marne can be found in *La Vie de Napoléon:* "Sooner or later, where military glory is concerned, one returns to marveling at the great things done with little means."

I think these maxims must be given further study, since Mérimée mentions them again, and "in position," as they say in the theater. There is decidedly much wisdom in this idea of maxims. Some claim that history endlessly repeats itself, others that it never does. That is not the problem. The truth is that men have no memory, and so each event takes them unawares, even if it has occurred a hundred times before. Maxims compensate for this lack of memory; they enable one to be ready for any eventuality, to face up to every surprise with an attitude as effective as if it were dictated by experience.

I have said (page 111) that a man without maxims is like a state without a policy. It would be more accurate to say a society without conventions, customs or morality. There are no such things as good or bad conventions; they are all equally valid. What matters is to maintain them, to hold by them. A conservative society is a powerful society. No rule, however absurd, is without its uses, for everyone tacitly conforms to it, and this tends to make communal life more uniform, more simple and more pleasant—the prime condition for an enduring society. Much fun has been made of the "proprieties," of court etiquette, of the fear of what the neighbors will say, and so on. But all that, laughable in itself, is indispensable to the community, otherwise nothing would subsist. The content lives only through the form just as the soul, in this world, lives only through the body. The forms have to be respected at all costs. What makes the strength and efficiency of a firm are the pernickety directors who have the letterhead reprinted five times and move their desks around for aesthetic reasons.

The finest example of the success of the conventions in society was, to my mind, the marriage of convenience, as this was understood from the seventeenth to the nineteenth centuries. The doctrine among families was that the children must be married to match their fortunes, and that love came later, if it came at all. A very wise conception, and victoriously opposing social morality (whose motto could be "Toward convenience by constraint") to natural morality. Little by little, natural morality has gained the upper hand and the institution of the love match, which seemed utterly irrational two centuries and even fifty years ago, has replaced the marriage of convenience. This doesn't lead to any happier marriages. Less happy, rather, for a man takes a wife as he does a mistress, tires of her in six months and divorces her the following year. In the marriage of convenience at least they cherished no illusions, and an inopportune love, whether exacting or unrequited, did not prevent friendship. From this I draw the motto of natural morality: "Toward constraint through convenience." In decadent societies, where natural morality generally replaces social morality, everyone is unhappy. Anarchy gives rise to a series of constraints much harsher than the most despotic authority.

A man with maxims is a man who believes that marriages of convenience are better than marriages for love. In other words, one must not yield to one's impulses, however seductive appearances may be; one must not live haphazardly. Mistrust of his emotions is the first precaution of a man of sensibility with an imagination that reacts strongly to events. What has once been true never ceases to be true, and one can always confront one's heart with it in delicate moments, unless one is absolutely determined to do something foolish.

The bridge over the Berezina before which Beyle and his colleague M. Bergonié stood provides a striking image. The man of maxims crosses the bridge. The man without remains gazing at it. He doesn't know that it is better to be in the vanguard of a retreating army than caught up in the flood of stragglers. He doesn't know that it is the rear guard that gets harried. A false conception of honor, as well: M. Bergonié, auditor to the Privy Council, had no business with the rear guard. That was the task of the officers of the forces bringing up the rear. At the Berezina, Beyle was twenty-nine. A cool man is cool at any age. In 1801, in Italy, he was no different. "What, is that all?" he asked himself after crossing the St. Bernard Pass. Shades of Fabrice! *Sang-froid* walks in step with the love of truth. It is rare for one to go without the other.

48

Like many men of his age, Beyle seemed to me to judge his contemporaries very harshly and my generation with a certain indulgence. He admired the taste for learning and eagerness to discover the true nature of things characteristic of young men in their twenties when he himself was forty. He would make gentle fun of our earnestness and pedantry, but used to say that we were no dupes, as they were in his day. Following his habit of making himself out to be worse than he was, he affected to despise the enthusiasm which had led his contemporaries to such great achievements. "We had the sacred flame," he used to say. "I, too, although unworthy. I was once sent to Brunswick to raise an extraordinary levy of five million francs. I got them to pay seven and was nearly annihilated by the rabble who rose in revolt, exacerbated by my excess of zeal. But the Emperor asked who the auditor was who was responsible for this and said, 'Well done.' "

O NE HARDLY UNDERSTANDS the word "youth" before one is thirty. The difference between the generations remained a dead letter for me until the moment when I was old enough suddenly to see a generation rising up behind my own— young men of twenty who hadn't received the same upbringing as I had or lived through the same events, or known the perils through which my contemporaries had passed. As I write this, I am the same age as Beyle was in 1821, when the Emperor died. But he belonged to a generation which had accomplished great things, which had reshaped the world; I and my like belong to a shabby generation, accustomed to defeat and dishonor. That rather alters one's outlook.

I don't exactly know what the men of my own age think of the young men who are twenty today. I don't believe I have ever raised this question with them. But, speaking only for myself, I find these young people much more attractive than those of 1940. They are austere, stubborn, brave, obliging, quite without irony and conscientious. "In *my* day" they pretended to be completely disillusioned and were blasé about everything, which is a sillier way than any other of being a dupe; more harmful, too, since it leads to passivity. I don't say that they are any less stupid now than before, but they are stupid in a less overwhelming, less contemptible way. The basic material is better. Compare, for instance, the army of 1958 with the one of 1939: a defeat like that of 1940 is no longer conceivable. Unlike Gamelin's great army, our little one of 1958 is full of valor. It would probably prefer death to defeat. It is doubtless true that a nation's spirit, that is to say its visage, changes every twenty years. In 1938, the youth of France had withdrawn from the world. In 1958, they have recovered the desire to influence it, to model it in their own image. It follows that I disliked the young men of 1938 and like those of today. A matter of taste.

These French soldiers would laugh and sing all day; they were all under twenty-five, and their general in command, who was twenty-seven, passed for the oldest man in his army. This gaiety, this youth, this insouciance provided an agreeable answer to the furious sermons of the monks, who for six months past had been announcing from aloft in the holy chair that the French were monsters, obliged under pain of death to burn everything and cut off everyone's head.

In these passionate terms Stendhal, at the beginning of *La Chartreuse*, evokes the army in Italy which entered Milan with Bonaparte on May 15, 1796. No youth has been so magnificently, so poetically hymned. But by 1804 it was all over. The generosity had crumbled away. They were out to become colonels or marshals. The youths in love with liberty and glory had become men preoccupied with their careers. And Napoleon, that "great heart," had become a liar.

It was not the same thing to be twenty in 1806 or 1809 as it was in 1796. The great and thrilling ideas of liberty, of the Republic, of happiness, had blurred over. But one could always be ambitious. The Emperor was there to reward the most impetuous and the most impatient. By 1820, ambition was no longer possible for the young. The lies of the Empire were addressed to boys who asked only to believe them, for they were imposing lies, accompanied by real glory. No glory counterbalanced the lies of the Restoration, and the young, whom the nation did not employ, had leisure to study and go to "the heart of things." This formed a rather earnest and pedantic generation, as Mérimée says, but a wise and thoughtful one which wouldn't let itself be imposed on. Add regret and nostalgia for having come into the world forty years too late, for having missed France's most stupendous adventure, for having attained manhood only to know defeat, capitulation, foreign occupation, self-abnegation, dishonor and weakness. I am well informed about this; I can answer for it. I have often regretted that I wasn't twenty in 1914 instead of 1940.

Referring to Armand Carrel, born in 1800, Littré has written a memorable phrase, surprising from the pen of so seemingly austere a man: "Brought up to be a soldier, he was what all the men of his generation were who had received a touch of the Empire's sun in their cradles." One never recovers from such a sunbath. But the youth of France bore the sunstroke of the Empire better than that of the victory of 1918.

It is to Beyle's credit that, though he had lived for twenty years with heroes and under the direction of a hero, he marveled at the children of the century instead of becoming crusty or a *laudator temporis acti*, like so many people. In *Brulard* he writes, "What distinguishes me from the self-important fools of the press, who carry their heads like a holy sacrament, is that I have never believed that society owed me the least thing." The soldier retired on half pay believes that society owes him something, even if only his full pay. The ex-serviceman believes that at least it owes him gratitude. The war ended, adventures over, Stendhal passed without difficulty or regret from military to civilian life, from brilliance to obscurity, from opulence to penury. At all events he still had one thing left—himself—and that was enough. Himself, which is to say an always contented but always shrewd observer of the ways of the world.

"We had the sacred flame," he says, as a manner of excuse, referring to the great deeds of the Revolution and the Empire. But even that alone is an explanation. There had been a revolution and an empire, and all that glory, because the French people had the "sacred flame." Reverse the terms: The sacred flame was in the French people; it wasn't the Empire, nor even the Revolution, that lit it. Patently, however, they kept it burning high. There seems nothing particular to be said on the way he "affected to despise the enthusiasm which had led his contemporaries to such great achievements." That is in Stendhal's manner. It is a meiosis, a civility toward his young companions, who had hardly any subjects around them over which to enthuse. The "I, too, although unworthy" is full of savor. It is akin to "You are a cat, I am a rat." I like to call this the ostentation of modesty. One finds such exaggerations among the most truly modest men.

"With the Emperor," says Stendhal in *Brulard*, "I was attentive, zealous, and never thought of my cravat, quite unlike the rest." Such is the serious, "although unworthy," man. To think of one's cravat is to think of oneself, of one's advancement. Not to think of it is to be concerned only with service, which is to say with one's country. Stendhal thought of his cravat only when those with cravats were in disarray: at the crossing of the Berezina, in 1812. Such are the reiterations of the noble soul. To do everything at the wrong time—that is how two contrary actions can have the same meaning.

Is it not strange to see Stendhal displaying zeal? And yet he did. How prodigious that period and the man who dominated it must have been to have brought him, Beyle, to that high peak of absurdity, importunity and presumption known as zeal! The affair of the seven million francs extorted from the Duchy of Brunswick is almost incredible. Seen from the standpoint of contemporary morals, it must appear monstrous to a whole class of people who, through indiscriminate humanitarianism, affect a denial of patriotism. Yet who was more cosmopolitan than Stendhal? But he also had what seems to be completely lacking in the consciences of 1958: *a scale of values*. In this scale, the success of the war and the strength of his own country came first.

And how is one to take the word "rabble," applied to the unhappy people of Brunswick, exacerbated by the extortions of M. l'Intendant? Such a word will stick in the throats of the left-wing Stendhalians, who naïvely believe that a man is all of one piece, that he never contradicts himself. The people today are so flattered and fawned on that the mildest word against them provokes instant indignation. Detesting all forms of superstition, I can no more understand this one than I can the rest. Why shouldn't one judge the people with the same impartiality as one does other groups or individuals? I can find as great faults in the people as in the bourgeoisie or the nobility. Stendhal found them in the same way, I imagine. The rabble doesn't exist only for gentlemen. Finally, I should like to recall this: Stendhal was a bourgeois of the beginning of the nineteenth century. He liked the rabble (a term of the period) as little as Voltaire did fifty years earlier, or Halévy forty years later. The term "rabble" covers many things—in particular, hatred of obscurantism, an aversion for unwashed people who are as obsequious as servants, as superstitious as children and unable to read. Doubtless all this will bring down a large part of the contemporary press about my ears. But attack your dear Stendhal first, please. It is he who talks of rabble, not I.

It was difficult to know what his feelings were toward Napoleon. He almost always held an opinion contrary to the one generally put forward. By turns scoffing and enthusiastic, at times he spoke of him as of an upstart dazzled by cheap glitter, ceaselessly failing to obey the rules of Lo-gic; at others, his admiration was almost idolatrous. By turns he was a scoffer like Courier and servile like Las Cases. The men of the Empire were treated as diversely as their master, but he agreed as to the fascination the Emperor wielded on everyone who approached him. He had begun a life of Napoleon, which was found among his papers. A fragment of this, vividly written, is to be found in his travels in France: the Emperor's arrival at Grenoble in 1815.

THIS VIVIDLY WRITTEN FRAGMENT (*Mémoires d'un Touriste*, August 27, 1837), includes the following sentence, which shows that Stendhal had as diverse opinions on the people as on Napoleon; speaking of a man who had raised his rifle to kill the Emperor, but did not fire for fear of seeing his wife and children lynched, he says, "Since there was energy in this action, it had for its author a man of the people." Show me a freer mind than Stendhal's. He sought to please no one, not even the people, not even the enemies of the people. That is the best way to please everybody. Such is the strange power of a truthful man in the long run. I say "in the long run" because, alas, he has to be dead first.

In the same fragment, Stendhal calls the return from Elba "the most romantic and beautiful enterprise of modern times." On that day, August 27, 1837, he had arranged to meet three peasants who had witnessed Napoleon's entry into Grenoble. "I must confess my childishness," he writes. "My heart was violently beating, I was deeply moved." The four of them lunched at the inn at Lafrey, near Grenoble. Several bottles of wine were consumed, but it was on enthusiasm that they got drunk. "After the enthusiasm of 1815," says Stendhal, "the French people sat back for fifteen years, and the most ignoble egoism prevailed everywhere." There you have the Restoration and the Revolution of 1830 judged by the man of sensibility.

Side by side with the man of sensibility, it is interesting to know what a man of politics, namely Chateaubriand, thought of the return from Elba: "There was in this fantastic conception a fierce egoism, a terrifying lack of gratitude and generosity toward France." But this man of politics was also a poet, who grasped what was invisible to the eyes of the historians. He adds:

> Comets describe curves which elude all calculations; they are tied to nothing, appear good for nothing; if some globe happens to be in their way, they shatter it and return into the abyss of the heavens; their laws are known only to God. Outstanding individuals are monuments of the human intellect; they are not its yardstick. Bonaparte was therefore less impelled to his undertaking by the false reports of his friends than by the demands of his genius; he embarked on his crusade by virtue of the faith he had in himself. For a great man it is not enough to be born— he has to die. Was the island of Elba an end for Napoleon?

The day after his meeting at Lafrey with the three peasants, Stendhal wrote the following, which I take the liberty of quoting in full, as it clearly reveals his feelings with regard to Napoleon. These seventeen lines contain an admirable summary of all the reasons for his admiration and mistrust.

I didn't want to read the official account Napoleon gave of this affair [his entry into Grenoble in 1815] until today, after my return to Grenoble; I found it perfectly correct. Napoleon had no reason to lie; besides, since this action was a great and fine one, he perhaps would not have wished to soil it by a lie, even when his interest as a despot would have counseled it. Often, the love this great-hearted man had for the noble got the better of his interest as a king. This can clearly be seen after the eighteenth Brumaire: scorn was often painted on his thin, well-carved lips at the appearance of those faithful and obsequious subjects who thronged to the levees at St.-Cloud. Is it only at this price that I can become emperor of the world? he seemed to be asking himself. And he encouraged servility. When, later on, he punished the generals who had shown spirit—Delmas, Lecourbe, etc., and the Jacobins—his feelings were different: he was afraid.

It is not at all hard today to know what feelings Napoleon inspired in Stendhal. He has left four or five most explicit pages, in which he admirably reveals the strength and weakness of this man who was always his hero, but whom he judged with the same inflexibility (and subtlety) as he put to judging a horse dealer, a colonel or a notary. It was left to him and Chateaubriand to give the most balanced and truthful portrait of Bonaparte. To Chateaubriand, he was a star, a dark sun; Stendhal cherished him to the point of treating him like one of his own characters. This is quite clear in his *Vie de Na-*

234

poléon; he describes him with tenderness, enthusiasm and lucidity, like some immense Julien Sorel.*

A man who sees the truth (and who has a spirit of contradiction) always tends to denigrate when others admire, and to exalt when others denigrate. Here are a few significant sentences from the preface to *La Vie de Napoléon:*

> I have tried not to be taken in. . . . My aim is to spread knowledge of this extraordinary man, whom I loved in his lifetime, whom I esteem now with all the contempt for what came after him. . . . Love of Napoleon is the one passion I have retained [written in 1837]; which doesn't prevent me from seeing the defects of his mind and the miserable weaknesses for which he can be reproached. . . . With me it is an almost instinctive belief that every man of power lies when he speaks, and with greater reason when he writes. . . . Napoleon revived the spirit of the French people; therein lies his truest glory.

In his *Journal,* under the date December 2, 1804, the day of the Emperor's coronation, Stendhal wrote:

> I reflected deeply all today on this manifest alliance of all the charlatans. Religion coming to consecrate tyranny and all that in the name of men's happiness. I rinsed my mouth by dipping into the prose of Alfieri.

I refer the reader again to the beautiful dedication of *L'Histoire de la peinture en Italie:* "To His Majesty Napoleon

---

* It is not always so easy to know exactly what Stendhal's feelings were toward Julien Sorel.

the Great, Emperor of the French, detained on the island of St. Helena . . ." It is signed "The soldier whom you took by the lapel at Goerlitz." One would like to quote everything Stendhal wrote on Napoleon. As space is limited and anyway the reader merely has to open *La Vie de Napoléon*, here is one final, astonishing quotation, referring to the skill with which the Emperor knew how to steer a conversation and never betrayed his ignorance on any subject: "This skill is perfectly echoed in the conversation of the savages, always careful of the opinion they may give of themselves." What an eye, to see Tamango in Bonaparte! He was there, no doubt, although very remote, at an incalculable depth, but Stendhal knew that to have energy one must preserve a trace of savagery in oneself.

It is the fashion today in France to vilify Napoleon and emphasize his more frightening aspects. A few years ago they almost gave serious consideration to a paltry book composed of the gossipings of subprefects and servants and tending to show that Napoleon was at heart just a very mediocre, vicious and mean little man. This compilation from the suspect memoirs of Barras, Bourrienne and others, would have been worthy of publication during the Restoration, when it was seriously maintained that Napoleon's real name was Nicolas. For myself, I must confess I cannot see what historical merit there can be in replacing the legend by tittle-tattle. I prefer the testimony of Stendhal and Chateaubriand to that of the valet Constant and even of Montholon. Only "great hearts" know how to speak of their equals.

Between Beyle and Napoleon one has the feeling of a formidable hierarchy, a prodigious distance. "The Emperor did not speak to lunatics like me," says Stendhal with combined mockery and modesty, struck by his littleness before the great man. He was fourteen years younger than his hero. At eighteen, in 1801, Stendhal had entered a society which was already beginning to call itself Bonapartean. It was a new state of things. After 1804, when Napoleon, by assuming the title of Emperor, "imprisoned his life in a grave comedy," the distance was no less great.

I myself have felt this odd impression of closeness or remoteness from the government, according to whether it is administered by incompetents or able men. With the former, who succeeded each other almost without a break from 1947 to 1958, it seemed to me that the government was in the street, within arm's reach, on a level with me. With de Gaulle, it has risen and receded to a great distance. Once again I regard it with the timidity and admiration I felt as a child whenever the President of the Republic was mentioned. Perhaps it is quite simply this feeling which explains the aversion one third of the country has for General de Gaulle; democratic habits and a taste for equality make one feel much more at ease under a discredited government made up of dishonest or incompetent men. To be at the head of the state and to be respectable— this almost seems too much to the French. They regard it as an insult, an unforgivable attack on their precious equality.

Unlike Stendhal, who reached manhood in a France which already possessed its hero, I myself, when I was twenty, saw a great man appear almost out of nowhere and suddenly raise himself to the stature of the world by a single word. This was de Gaulle, in June 1940. The act of a great heart, which gave infinite delight to the proud of spirit.

Judging by Beyle's stories, it seems to me that at the time of his youth there was less egoism than there is today, and that the fashionable affectations were of a nobler nature. Thus Beyle, although he loved good cheer, carefully refrained from admitting it. He even considered the time one spends in eating as time lost and expressed a wish that by swallowing a pill in the morning one could be rid of hunger for the whole day. Nowadays people are gluttons and boast of it. In Beyle's time, a man laid claim above all to energy and courage. How can one go through a campaign if one is a gastronome?

O tempora, o mores! Brillat Savarin has had a more lasting influence in France than Robespierre. For a hundred years cooking has been the one preoccupation. This topic of conversation bores me. Is there not pride in the talk of the great French eaters? They sing the praises of *pâté de grives, boeuf à la ficelle,* Chambertin and *Blanc de blancs* just as the war veterans do of the Chemin des Dames or Verdun. Drivel for drivel, I prefer a Slice of Bayonets to *quenelles de brochet.* It is more noble. Heroism is a grand style, gluttony a little one. I also seem to remember that gluttony is one of the seven deadly sins. If it is not perhaps the mother of all the vices, it is at least the patent manifestation of some ugly tendencies. Mérimée speaks of egoism. One might in this connection cite the famous parallel of the well-fed and starving nations and recall that it is the latter which model the world. To be a glutton is to think a great deal about one's body and thereby to forget one's soul.

It is not surprising that Stendhal, who thought only of his soul, should advocate pills. It is true that the time one spends in eating is time lost. Lost for less coarse pleasures, lost for passion. This was Napoleon's opinion; it is the opinion of all men of any ardor, who gulp down their lunch in ten minutes, heedless of what they are served. One of the few good features of the Anglo-Saxon countries is that one eats so badly in them, with almost no regard for mealtimes; their inhabitants despise food and regard it as a necessary bore. What could be more frightful than those annihilating lunch parties in which the French indulge at the slightest excuse and which one leaves thickheaded and weak at the knees, stupefied with meat and wine, incapable of a single idea until the evening?

Nations that gormandize are ripe for slavery. They bury their souls in fat. The plump, prosperous and well-fed France was subdued in a trice by the thin S.S. of 1940. These remarks will appear oversimplified, and I shall be taken to task for daring to impinge on French intestines, which are sacred; even so, I am only repeating a historical law which has been demonstrated a hundred times: "How can one go through a campaign if one is a gastronome?" Energy and courage don't go with a constant preoccupation over eating well. In the armies of the Revolution they thought only of their souls; a little less, but still a great deal, in those of the Empire. I suppose this generosity re-emerged between 1914 and 1918. During the famine of 1940-45, the soul appeared naked once again and provoked a number of fine deeds.

Is it not amusing in this paragraph to read Mérimée's attitude toward his contemporaries? It is the opposite of Stendhal's two paragraphs above. "There was less egoism than there is today," he says. He had written, "Beyle seemed to me to judge his contemporaries very severely." This shows (but unwittingly) that men of sensibility (Mérimée perfectly deserves this qualification, whatever people may think) are always ill at ease among their own generation.

51

Beyle loved intimate gatherings of just a few people. In a small circle, surrounded by friends or people to whom he felt well disposed, he happily gave a free rein to all the gaiety inherent in his character. He never set out to dazzle, only to enjoy himself and amuse others, "For," he used to say "one has to pay for one's admission." Always in high spirits, he was sometimes rather wild, indeed even indecent; but he set us all laughing, so that it was impossible for the prudish to keep a straight face. The presence of a bore or a spiteful wit froze him and promptly put him to flight. He never learned the art of knowing how to be bored. He used to say that life is short and that the time wasted in yawning can never be regained. He greatly admired M. de M——'s bon mot that "bad taste leads to crime."

M. DE M—— was M. de Mareste, whom Stendhal honors with several pages in his *Souvenirs d'égotisme*, from which he does not emerge as a very sympathetic character. It would be hard to find two men more dissimilar than Stendhal and Mareste. But there are times when one grows attached to a person with whom one has nothing in common, just as one gets used to an uncomfortable piece of furniture and ends by preferring it to any other. It is the discomfort that one likes, the constraint, the sharp corners which pleasurably hurt you; a little ugliness, too, does no harm. These strange attachments are hardly to be explained, except by a sort of abandonment to fatalism. One might rationalize them roughly as follows:

"Heaven has placed in my path such a man or piece of furniture; as much this one as any other. I never sought it, nor did he or it seek me. This meeting is the work of fate. Let us be somewhat superstitious. Let us obey. Experience teaches us that what one has earnestly wished for is seldom better than what comes our way by chance."

Here is a paragraph from Stendhal depicting the Baron de Mareste:

> M. de M——, short, sturdy, thickset, unable to see more than ten feet, always badly dressed out of avarice and spending our walks together making budgets of personal expenses for a fellow living alone in Paris, had a rare sagacity. In my romantic and dazzling illusions I saw as thirty, when they rated only fifteen, the genius, goodness, glory, happiness of some man who passed by, whereas he saw them as only six or seven. This is what formed the basis of our conversation for eight years; we sought each other out from one end of Paris to the other.

For eight years Stendhal and Mareste saw each other twice a day. Every morning at ten-thirty they met at the Café de Rouen. Mareste made himself guilty of two cardinal faults. Firstly he assumed airs of superiority on account of a private income of 22,000 francs which he had, arrogantly handing out advice and showing a faint contempt for Beyle; secondly, he supplanted his friend in the favors of Mme. Azur, that is, Alberthe de Rubempré, "a whore not sublime, à la Du Barry," but also "one of the least doll-like of Frenchwomen" that Stendhal had ever met.*

---

* As a counterpart to the traitor Mareste, here is the true friend: By dint of talking about Mme. Azur to Mérimée, and about him to her, Beyle had made these two fall in love with each other. This drove him to despair. Having shortly to leave Paris, he begged Mérimée to "spare his grief" for just two weeks more. "Two years, if you like," replied Mérimée. "I've

All these features of Mareste's are ugly. Superiority toward one's friends is an unforgivable crime. And the deceit is hardly more excusable. The oddest thing is the way in which Stendhal broke with him: he changed his café without saying a word. Mareste never asked for an explanation. These great changes, which happen like this without a word being said, always amaze me, even though I have experienced them or provoked them myself. In point of fact, they complete ruptures which have begun much earlier but remained invisible or carefully concealed. No doubt people frequently grow cool toward each other at the same pace. Stendhal says that Mareste began to adopt a superior attitude in about the seventh year of their friendship and that a further year went by before he determined to leave the Café de Rouen for the Café Lemblin. One year of silence is worth three hours of explanations.

The Baron's bon mot which I admire, that "bad taste leads to crime," gives a good idea of his intellect, wit, even profundity, and helps one to understand the pleasures of conversation (the keenest to be found) that Stendhal enjoyed with him. Vauvenargues has said something rather similar, but less well: "One must have feeling to have taste." Mareste goes further and deeper; his mot is more striking and more true.

On Stendhal's reactions to society, I have the following observation to make: It must not be forgotten that the man of wit masks the man of sensibility. The latter shies at a nothing, at the most imperceptible sign of hostility. The moment a shadow falls across a sensitive spirit, the wit takes flight and he sits foolish, morose and silent in the midst of the most delightful company. In order to shine (and his brilliance is incomparably brighter than any other) the man of sensibility needs

---

lost all taste for Madame de Rubempré since I saw her stockings hanging like concertinas round her legs."

Many will consider this coarse or brutal. I see it as an example of perfect delicacy, the authentic hallmark of a man of sensibility.

affection, a certain complicity from those present and, failing admiration, at least respect. Without this, he folds up his petals like a four-o'clock.

Everything in this paragraph is significant: the gaiety inherent in his character, enjoying himself and amusing others, people to whom he felt well disposed, friends, growing a bit wild and indecent, as one is with friends, laughing and causing laughter. "One has to pay for one's admission" is the maxim of an unpretentious man who does not arrive with his fame going before him, and who knows that nothing is due to him. (Is that possibly the definition of "kindliness"?) A bore or a spiteful wit is quite enough to poison the pleasures of a man of sensibility and put him to flight, for then everything is interpreted against him; otherwise he must control himself, revert to hypocrisy and lies. With a spiteful wit, there is no more freedom in conversation, no more lack of restraint. One is a man under arrest, best advised to say nothing until one's lawyer is present. There are people who never say anything dangerous and whose every word, precisely, seems to have been weighed by an interior jurist who always warns them if there is risk of being sued. This wasn't the case with Stendhal, who said no matter what, the moment it was dictated by the gaiety of his character and because this gaiety gave happiness. All in all, this is a healthy outlook, for it is better to be imprudent and happy than prudent and unhappy.

He was perfectly aware of his inability to be bored. With a man who sincerely puts happiness above everything else, and who demands an effervescence of the spirit as often as possible, it is quite true that "time wasted in yawning is never regained," since he yawns for nothing. No post, no pension, no medal compensates later on for his yawns. There is no reason for being bored when one is not ambitious. Life is short. The essential is that it should be *well filled*. Filled with a large number of moments of happiness.

Honesty was one of the hallmarks of Beyle's character. No one could be more loyal or reliable to deal with. I have never known a man of letters more frank in his criticisms, or more gallant in accepting those of his friends. He loved to pass around his manuscripts and would ask for them to be severely annotated. However harsh or even unjust the comments made, he never took offense at them. It was one of his maxims that whoever makes a profession of putting black on white must be neither surprised nor offended when told that he is a fool. This maxim he followed to the letter and, for his part, it was in no sense indifference, either real or affected. Criticisms preoccupied him greatly; he would dispute them keenly, but without acerbity and as if they concerned the works of an author who had been dead for several hundred years.

THIS PARAGRAPH leaves me with an unpleasant impression: it smacks of Sainte-Beuve. In his *Lundi* on Stendhal I find: "Beyle had a fundamental honesty and soundness in his personal relations which one could never forget to acknowledge even when one had told him a few home truths." Certainly where Sainte-Beuve is malicious, Mérimée is not so. Sainte-Beuve smothers the writer under the man, as it always suited him to do when attacking a true talent. Yet the two expressions seem to be akin and I sense in Mérimée a trace of Sainte-Beuve's condescension.

Proust has finally and forever condemned the method of

Sainte-Beuve, who claimed that a work is explained by the life of the man who produced it. It is astounding that so keen a wit should have fallen into such a howling error. A work of art cannot be reduced to anything. It rises up out of a truly fathomless abyss. Sainte-Beuve's method, says Proust,

> fails to recognize what a familiarity of any depth with ourselves teaches us: that a book is a product of another self than the one we display in our habits, in society, in our vices. This self, if we wish to try to understand it, can be attained only in our innermost hearts, by trying to recreate it within us. Nothing can exempt us from this effort of our hearts. We must make this truth out of nothing and it is all too easy to believe that it will come to us one fine morning, in the mail, in the form of an unpublished letter sent to us by some librarian we know, or that we shall pluck it from the lips of someone who knew the author well.

To put it briefly, the man who writes is not the man who lives. Naturally, life nourishes the work, but in a subtle way. The organism of the artist transforms the nourishment following processes incomprehensible to the critics.

When one reads Sainte-Beuve, one is filled with indignation three times on every page. So many subtle and ingenious ideas put to serve this aberrant method! Balzac, before Proust, had seen the flaw in this butterfly collector's criticism. He rightly laughed at Sainte-Beuve, "who writes biographies of unknown men." It is, in effect, to writing biographies of unknown men that the desire to be a historian (or chronicler) at all costs leads. At this Sainte-Beuve was incomparable. And that is understandable; Mme. Gasparin, Charles de Bernard, Vinet, Molé, Mme. de Verdelin, Ramond and Vicq-d'Azyr all led lives that are delightful to describe. There is no mystery in the works of these good folk, and the events which gave birth to their wan volumes are far more interesting than what they drew from them. But Stendhal? What can explain *La Chartreuse?* Neither the consul nor the lover, nor the student of music; not the shrewd politician, nor the man of wit. It came from other depths. The lives of artists have something in common with both the lives of saints and the lives of heroes. In other words, there is in them an irrational "factor of superiority," which ungifted people must resolve never to penetrate. The lives of the saints reveal a constant application to saintliness. In the lives of heroes, it is not unusual to see five or six great deeds cutting across a mediocre life, a mean character, sometimes even knavishness. And so I hold that the lives of artists derive from both of these; a constant application to art does not necessarily affect a man's morals, and one often meets superb artists who have but tiny souls.

At the age of eighteen, I was enabled to prove the folly of Sainte-Beuve's method on myself. At that time I kept a most sincere diary, in which I scrupulously and exactly noted down my most secret feelings and my most surprising thoughts. At the same time, I composed sonnets whose inspiration derived from Mallarmé, featuring Orpheus, Salome, Apollo or Icarus. One day it struck me that my antique sonnets and jangling verses revealed more about myself, my innermost self, my metaphysical self, than my diary, in which I indulged in shameless and reckless self-analysis. I realized that day that art is quite a different thing from veracious little comments on life or, if you prefer it, well-written journalism. In spite of their subject matter, my lack of skill, my absurd aesthetic, there was in my poems a sort of music, a song which was the very expression of what I did not as yet know of my soul, of all that I subsequently learned to know without seeking to understand.

". . . As if they concerned the works of an author who

had been dead for several hundred years." In his *Contre Sainte-Beuve*, a posthumous work first published in 1954, Proust, in his way, defined the philosophy of this attitude of Stendhal's: The man who writes being not the same as the man who lives, the duality operates in both directions. When one has finished writing, one returns to life, one changes souls. If need be, a writer should be able to judge his own works as he does someone else's. Such detachment is rare, but even so not impossible. Stendhal is there to prove it.

This demands a rare strength, complete honesty, and above all an almost infallible understanding of one's art, thanks to which one senses immediately and unerringly what is fair criticism and what is not. Addressed to such a man, all criticism is useful or, at worst, unimportant. I know of no one more ludicrous or odious than the writer whose whole attitude proclaims, "Whoever likes me likes my books." It puts me in mind of old suburban ladies whose maxim is "Love me, love my dog."

I know many who could profit from Stendhal's maxim that whoever makes a profession of putting black on white must be neither surprised nor offended when told that he is a fool, beginning with myself, since I feel a keen animosity for the critics who condemn my writings for bad reasons (or who praise them for what are in fact their defects, which is the same thing). After all, it is we writers who set the ball rolling, who "submit the fruits of our labor to the judgment of the public." Nobody asks us to do this, and, as Stendhal says, nobody owes us anything, since society pays only for the services it sees. The greatest services are free, for they are always invisible. Therein lies their charm for the man who renders them. Good writers know this perfectly well and profit from it with interest.

He had adopted the odd habit of surrounding his most everyday activities with mystery, in order to baffle the police, whom he in all likelihood believed to be simple enough to pay attention to salon gossip. He never wrote a letter without signing it with a fictitious name: César Bombet, Cotonet, and so on; he would date it from Abeille instead of Civitavecchia and would often begin with such a sentence as "I have received your raw silks and have stored them pending shipment." The notes he ceaselessly took were like riddles, and he himself was often at his wit's end to guess their meaning when they dated back several days.

It must be fairly admitted that in this little essay Mérimée does not follow a very strict order and often repeats himself. This disadvantage does not occur in *H.B.* But I have given the reasons for having chosen this text rather than *H.B.* If thereby construction suffers and I am obliged to be untidy, even in turn to repeat myself, it can't be helped. Thanks to repetitions one sometimes discovers new points of view. Mérimée and I have already spoken of the police and Beyle's mysteries. But here is something that is new in one aspect. Unlike Mérimée, and just like Stendhal, I believe that the police are indeed simple enough to pay attention to salon gossip. This is because Stendhal and I were not twenty years old at the same time as Mérimée, and we have known other circumstances. When I was twenty, the police were everywhere and their omnipresence made me, as it did Stendhal, invincibly mistrustful. Even today I see them everywhere, ingratiating or brutal, taking their notes on everything in a clumsy (that is to say, slanderous) style.

Once they are acquired, one never rids oneself of secretive habits. Even so, I imagine that Stendhal's notes to which Mérimée alludes referred to true facts or petty occurrences and were not concerned with ideas; for however elliptical or abbreviated the form an author gives them, he cannot be mistaken on rereading them. In support of this, I hope I shall be forgiven for reproducing an experiment I made when I was about eighteen, which was one of the first of my calling as a writer: My diary became a notebook, a memorandum pad. I often reread it, sure of finding in it the traces of true sensations, manifest thoughts. Certainly, I recorded there only the high point of a sensation, the final outcome of an argument, the most intimate things that stirred the deepest parts of the heart, but it was honest, and it was easy to trace the road back, to redescend to the prime causes. The route was a good one: from the interior to the exterior. In this way and without the least difficulty I could work my way back into states of mind six months old or more. I had in fact glued the words and the spirit together. I expressed things as precisely as possible, for I was recording the moment, and, having recorded it, I could forget without fear. Therefore I had thought, felt, only a very brief moment. It needed great exactitude to feel or think the same thing on a simple reading six months later.

I think that Stendhal feared the eyes of the indiscreet as much as the police. When one practices γνῶθι σεαυτόν in writing one exposes oneself to the curiosity of imbeciles who never fail to go and delve among your papers when you are out* and afterward use your most private confessions against

---

* Or dead.—P.

you. I don't mean by this that Stendhal need have blushed for the slightest thing he wrote about his heart or his life, but he knew that the confidences of the sensitive are always misinterpreted by the vulgar who chance on them, and that what is merely a curious, exciting or instructive truth becomes, when seen through their eyes, exhibitionism, cynicism, remorse or boasting. Such are the disadvantages of being sincere with oneself. I once knew a doctor who kept his private diary in Greek so that his housekeeper shouldn't read it. Leonardo da Vinci wrote from right to left.

One can never be too cautious when one loves truth and is an expert at the art of catching it in flight. Truth is as dangerous a possession as the rarest of state secrets. As we know, it has cost many people their lives or their honor.

He had no fear of death, but did not like to speak of it, holding it to be something dirty and ugly rather than terrible. He had the one he desired, the one that Caesar had wished for: Repentinam inopinatamque.

M ARCEL PROUST, in *Sodome et Gomorrhe*, has M. de Charlus say, "I no longer remember which man of taste replied, to someone who asked him what event had afflicted him most in his life, 'The death of Lucien de Rubempré in *Splendeurs et Misères.*'" To each man his heroes. For me, the death of Lucien de Rubempré seems contemptible, like his life, and I am less sensitive than M. de Charlus, no doubt, to a queer kind of poetry. On the other hand, I haven't read *Le Rouge* for seven years because of the death of Julien Sorel. It drives me too close to despair. In the same way, I am deeply affected by the death of Stendhal. Whenever I think of it, it spreads a cloud of sorrow over my thoughts. The evening of March 22, 1842, seems to me a black day for mankind, because it saw the sensitive spirit of Henri Beyle pass away. Such regrets are absurd, I know, and Stendhal would have had to die sooner or later, long before my birth; but we are as we are, and it is beyond my power not to brood sadly over the death of someone of whom, like Mérimée, I can say, "Few men have pleased me more."

Everyone knows the circumstances of this death. Stendhal

was fifty-nine. He fell in a fit of apoplexy on the pavement of the Rue Neuve-des-Capucines. Some passers-by picked him up. "As a result of purely fortuitous circumstances," wrote his cousin Romain Colomb, "I was beside my unfortunate friend twenty minutes after it happened. I found him lying unconscious in a shop opposite the spot where he had fallen. I couldn't get one word or the smallest sign out of him. He was carried to his lodging in the Rue Neuve-des-Petits-Champs. There all the resources of medical skill were applied without success, and he breathed his last on Wednesday, March 23, at two in the morning, without any suffering, without having spoken a single word, at the age of fifty-nine years, one month and twenty-eight days."

There exists a little manuscript by Stendhal called *Les Privilèges*, arranged in twenty-three articles, in which he sets out all sorts of grave and gay fantasies which, he thinks, would represent for him happiness on earth. It begins like this: "God gives me the following commission: 'Article I: Never any serious pain until an advanced old age; then, not pain, but death by apoplexy, in bed, while asleep, without any moral or physical pain.'" Colomb has added the following note to the manuscript: "Every time Beyle spoke of death, he expressed a desire for his life to end by a fit of apoplexy during sleep, while traveling, in a village inn. This wish, so often expressed, was fulfilled, at least according to its main condition, on March 22, 1842."

In 1841 Stendhal had written, "I find there is nothing ridiculous about dying in the street when one doesn't do it on purpose." Doesn't this, so typical of his manner, bring tears to the eyes? One last, infinitely touching thing: He wanted a grave with a view. But he never had one. Colomb wasn't rich enough to offer him this last pleasure.

I recall the passage in *Lamiel* where that beautiful girl, in order to make herself ugly and so avoid being plagued by the attentions of common men, smeared her face with holly green. This makes a good allegory for Stendhal. All his life he smeared holly green on his soul to conceal its beauty.

About the Author

JEAN DUTOURD *was born in 1920. He studied philosophy at the Sorbonne, was called up in 1940 and was taken prisoner soon afterward. He escaped by jumping off the train on his way to Germany and joined the resistance movement. In 1943 he was caught by the Gestapo and sentenced to death, but again he escaped and resumed his underground activities.*

M. Dutourd writes for numerous French and Swiss newspapers. He is also on the staff of a French publishing house. He is married and has two children. The Man of Sensibility *is his thirteenth book and the fifth to be translated into English.*